WINDS OF CHANGE IN A SLEEPY SUSSEX VILLAGE (RUSTINGTON)

By

Graeme Taylor

and

Mary Taylor BEM

WINDS OF CHANGE IN A SLEEPY SUSSEX VILLAGE

(Rustington)

By

Graeme Taylor & Mary Taylor BEM

ISBN: 978-0-9933555-0-9

This book is published by Graeme Taylor and Mary Taylor in conjunction with **WRITERSWORLD**, and is produced entirely in the UK. It is available to order from most bookshops in the United Kingdom, and is also globally available via UK based Internet book retailers.

WRITERSWORLD
2 Bear Close Flats, Bear Close, Woodstock
Oxfordshire, OX20 1JX, England
☎ 01993 812500
☎ +44 1993 812500

www.writersworld.co.uk

The text pages of this book are produced via an independent certification process that ensures the trees from which the paper is produced come from well managed sources that exclude the risk of using illegally logged timber while leaving options to use post-consumer recycled paper as well.

CONTENTS

INTRODUCTION

The idea or inspiration for writing this book came originally from a conversation my paternal grandfather had with my father in 1935. He apparently told my dad that they should send me to the East Street School in Littlehampton (now the Flintstone Centre) when I became five years old rather than attending my local school, the Rustington Church School.

Apparently my grandfather did not want me to be brainwashed into praising Adolf Hitler and all he was hoping to achieve in making Europe a better place as was seemingly happening to some of the pupils here in Rustington School.

Of course, I knew nothing of this until I was married and had two sons of my own, when one day my father told me all about it.

I always wondered why, as a five year old, I was sent off to the East Street School in Littlehampton on the number 31 bus, all on my own after the first week, instead of attending the local school, just a short walk away, as of course most of the other local children did.

It was on the 5th October, 2013 that Graeme and I first started to discuss the idea of doing this book as a joint project. We remember the date well as we had gone to see a wonderful candlelit concert, at Trading Boundaries at Fletching in East Sussex, performed by Thijs Van Leer from our favourite band Focus amidst a backdrop of Roger Dean's original paintings. It was during the interval that we started discussing ideas for the new book.

So having undertaken intensive research with my son Graeme, I can now see, all those years ago, why I was sent to school in Littlehampton.

Focus playing live at Trading Boundaries (1)

Focus prior to concert at Trading Boundaries. (2) From left to right:

Roger Dean (artist); Pierre van der Linden; Bobby Jacobs; Thijs van Leer; Menno Gootjes; Steve Hackett (former member of Genesis); Tracy Thompson and Michael Clifford (co-owners of Trading Boundaries).

Mary pictured here with Thijs van Leer.
(They share the same birthday.) (3)

Whilst completing the research it became apparent that, given the title we had chosen, there were other important characters and changes in the village that we wanted to concentrate on. Graeme became especially interested in the Suffrage movement and the Garretts in particular and endeavoured to find out more.

This book is the result of our studies together.

THE SLEEPY VILLAGE

The sleepy village in question is Rustington in West Sussex, to be found about halfway along the coast between Chichester and Brighton.

Rustington has often been referred to as a sleepy village in the past and some people will say it still is today.

If you can actually find a mention of the village in books about Sussex you'll be lucky. When you do they will consist of just a few lines. This has not changed much since the turn of the 20th Century.

Sea Road looking east towards the windmill and the southern end of Sea Lane. (4)

One such entry is to be found in *The Sussex Coast* which states: "About two miles south-west of Lyminster is the once quiet little village of Rustington, close to the sea. There is a windmill by the shore; once it was a lonely spot, now villas and bungalows are growing up, there is a large Metropolitan Asylums' Home, and a motor road full of sharp little flints leads along the seaside to Littlehampton." (Hannah, 1912)

In 2014, the population of the village has swelled to around 14,000 and is set to rise again in the coming years. The area is 3.72km² (1.44 sq. mi.) with a population density of around 10,000 per square mile. The village now has no fields or woodland areas and possesses just a minute amount of green space or recreational facilities.

According to the 1881 census the village had a total of 71 occupied houses, nine unoccupied, four houses being built and one shed or hut in occupation, with a total of 360 residents! In 1891, the total had risen to 91 properties.

Scattered around the village there were farmers, bricklayers, millers, wheelwrights, carpenters, ex-military personnel, labourers etc. The only shop was a post office in Sea Lane run by the baker and greengrocer, Mary Ann Humphrey.

Mary Ann Humphrey's post office and shop, the only shop in the village at that time. (5)

Other notable residents in situ at the time the census was taken were Hugh Penfold, a barrister at Rustington House;

William Lawler, the headmaster at School House; and Edmund Stansfield, the vicar. Living at Seafield Court was the Dowager Lady Frances Armstrong who was the mother-in-law of Dame Nellie Melba.

At this time the owners of the larger residences would often be away from their houses, along with their servants, at properties owned by them in London and elsewhere, or visiting family or taking part in other social engagements both in England and abroad.

Villagers awaiting a carnival procession in 1913. (6)

Many of the richer families had more than one residence, usually one in London and one or more in the country. So in the census many of the larger houses were recorded as unoccupied. The owners of these properties were as follows:

At The Marigolds lived Mary Dundas Hamilton, daughter of John Hamilton and Kathryn Barbara Stobart. The family owned Sundrum Castle in Ayrshire as did their ancestors.

At Cudlow House lived Andrew MacFarlane and his wife Flora (nee MacFarlane); she was the daughter of James and Irma. Irma was part of the Gaillard family of Balembouche who owned a sugar plantation in St. Lucia.

We now move onto The Grange, where Richard Denny Urlin (of Huguenot descent) and his wife Mary Elizabeth (nee Addis) lived with their four children, namely, Ethel Lucy Hargreave (born 23rd June 1858); Maud Radcliffe (born 21st July 1860); Amy Agnes (born 21st January 1865) all in Rustington and Hilda Mary Isabel (born 8th June 1871) in Dublin. They sadly lost their first daughter Lilian Mary (born 9th September 1856) on 25th January 1857.

Richard was an eminent barrister, living in Ireland for many years. In 1880 he wrote *A Churchman's Life of Wesley* along with many legal textbooks. His wife Mary edited a very interesting account of his life entitled *The Journal and Reminiscences of R. Denny Urlin*, published in 1909.

Left: Richard Denny Urlin and his wife Mary Elizabeth standing outside their home The Grange. (7)

Looking down Sea Lane from the Parish Church with The Grange on the left-hand side. (8)

During Richard Denny Urlin's time here he spoke eloquently to the members and friends of the Robin Society, which had recently been formed in the village. This society was a precursor to the RSPB. The Society for the Protection of Birds was founded in 1889 to counter the horrendous trade in plumes for women's hats, a fashion in the late Victorian era which saw the destruction of many thousands of birds such as birds of paradise, egrets, great crested grebes, kittiwakes and other species. These early societies consisted entirely of women as they were distraught by the plight of young birds being left to starve in the nest following their parents being shot for their plumage.

The following short account of the inaugural meeting of the local society in Rustington was published in the *Littlehampton News* on September 15th, 1891.

Robin Society at Rustington

The inaugural meeting of a local society lately formed under the name of the Robin Society, was held in the Parochial Schoolroom on the evening of September 7th. When there was a very full attendance of members and friends of the Society. There were songs and recitations, and an address was then given by Mr Richard Denny Urlin, the eminent Barrister, on the obligations of Man towards the lower animals, and especially to the feathered creation. He referred to the touching and beautiful language employed by the poets, chiefly by Cowper, Coleridge and Wordsworth, (whose birthday it was). He deprecated wanton injury such as bird nest robbing. It was stated that the new society (formed for the protection of birds and the discouragement of cruelty) already numbered many members. The meeting closed with a vote of thanks to the Lady who had founded the Society, and with the National Anthem. (*Littlehampton News*, 1891)

Ethel Urlin was to later write in 1909 *The Memorials of the Urlin Family*. In 1914, she was the Honorary Secretary of the first ever rural branch, here in Rustington, of the Women's Volunteer Reserve, commanded by Viscountess Castlereagh. The Honorary Colonel was Lady French, the wife of Field Marshall Sir John French who was appointed the Chief of Staff of the British Army from 1911 and then Commander of the British Expeditionary Force in 1914. However, he was temperamentally unsuited to this command which resulted in him being replaced by his deputy, Douglas Haig.

Maud Radcliffe married Frank Hesketh Peters, author of *The Nicomachean Ethics of Aristotle*.

In October 1897, the Urlin family thoughts were much taken up that autumn with the engagement and marriage of Hilda with Professor Flinders Petrie of the University College, London. On November 29th 1897, the marriage took place at the Parish Church, Kensington, at 9am (it was all over by 9.50am). The couple went off from the vestry door to Victoria Station, en-route for Calais, Paris and Egypt. Twelve of the family sat down to breakfast at 10.30am and some of them went on to the Tate Gallery later on.

Flinders was an eminent English Egyptologist and he was to

become a pioneer in the systematic methodology in archaeology and the preservation of artefacts. The Petrie Museum, which has over 80,000 artefacts, is part of University College London Museum and Collections. Part of this collection was kept in a store room (large shed) in Seafield Road, roughly where the Smugglers, as it is known to the locals, stands today. (It is now the Dragon Restaurant.) Hilda was also an English Egyptologist (as was her sister Amy, who would often go to Egypt with them). (Urlin, 1909)

Professor & Mrs Flinders Petrie at Abydos, Egypt in 1900. (9)

Most of the members of the family, including their spouse and offspring, spent a lot of time away from Rustington; however, they were always glad to come back to the village.

Our lovely ancient Parish Church here in Rustington has a series of extremely fine 19th and early 20th Century stained glass windows. At least one of these windows is dated and signed by Thomas Figgis Curtis in 1907.

After Thomas's wife Mary Curtis died, one of his stained glass windows was dedicated to her; later, after Thomas died, a further dedication was added for him. "*To the glory of God § in loving memory of Mary Curtis 1847-1921 §of Thomas Curtis 1844-1924."* (Sadly, in 1983, a wanton act of desecration occurred when a tombstone was broken off and thrown through the bottom half of this stained glass window. It has since been repaired using information and photographs supplied by us.)

Thomas Curtis came to Rustington originally in the 19th Century to fulfil a commission, to make and install stained glass windows in the church for the then vicar, The Reverend Edmund Stansfield.

It is probable that all the unsigned windows were made by the company which Thomas Curtis owned, called Curtis, Ward and Hughes. This company employed over 100 men and was situated at 67 Frith Street on the corner of Soho Square in London.

We believe that on his earliest visit to Rustington he noticed a flint-faced house for sale called Walnut Tree House, which he immediately fell in love with and bought for his family in 1887. This house is possibly the earliest of all the ancient houses in Rustington.

It would certainly appear to have been adapted from a typical timber-framed hall house (an example of a hall house can be seen at the Singleton Open Air Museum).

Dating from the 15th Century, Walnut Tree House was at this time a working farm with its lands running down almost as far as the sea and east as far as Firs Cottage. Over time more and more land was sold off, but the house was enlarged and changed, including having flint facing etc. The last portion of land to be sold was where Walnut Tree Avenue and Ingram Close now run.

An interesting book has been written about the Curtis family including Thomas and Mary's two daughters, Ethel and Dora. Tragically, Dora died young but Ethel, in 1900, made a disastrous marriage to Gilbert Kibblewhite. He appears to have been a very violent man and after their second child was born the marriage ended.

The two children of their marriage were Diana and Peter. The story of Diana has been expertly written and illustrated by Thea Abbott and is called *Diana Poulton – The Lady with the Lute*. I was very privileged to have been asked about her and other local celebrities in the village about the time of this story as well as supplying photographs of Walnut Tree House. (Poulton, 2013)

Carrying on our trek around the village...

We found an interesting note from *The News & South Coast Visitors Journal*, dated Wednesday Oct 26th, 1887. It concerns one of the residents listed above.

A dispatch from Brussels gives particulars of a new debutante, who must be known to some Littlehampton & Rustington people.

Her stage name is Madam Melba; her domestic appellation is Mrs Armstrong. She is a young and attractive Soprano, wife of a wealthy Australian, and made a sensational debut, at the Theatre de la Monnaie on Friday night, in the role of Gilda (Rigoletto – An opera in 3 acts by Verdi). The new Prima Donna, who hails from Melbourne, had an enthusiastic reception and her appearance is regarded as a great artistic event. Her voice is powerful and singularly pure and crystalline in quality, fully equal according to the many connoisseurs who applauded her, to Patti, in her younger days. Madam Melba and her husband were staying at Seafield Court Rustington, last summer, with Mr Armstrong's Mother. (*The News & South Coast Visitors Journal*, 1887)

Another item, this from *The Littlehampton News* in October 1893, mentions many of the local residents living in the village at that time.

Opening of the new Rustington Reading Room

On Saturday last a Reading Room was formally opened at Rustington by Mrs Wellesley of that village. The building, situated between Jessamine Cottage and the Vinery, is a wooden structure and is very well fitted.

Left: Coin struck by the Perth Mint. (10)

Right: Dame Nellie Melba. (11)

Mr Andrew Macfarlane took the chair, and was supported by Mr and Mrs Gerald Wellesley, Mrs Day, the Misses Parry, the Misses Macfarlane, Mrs Urlin, the Misses Urlin, Miss Agnes Garrett, Mrs & Miss Curtis, Mrs Macdonald, the Misses Macdonald and Miss Thorn.

Mr Macfarlane in opening the meeting said, "That in opening a room of such description in such a small village as sleepy Rustington, they might pat themselves on the back. Very few villages of such size could boast of a similar room, so that after all they were not so very sleepy. The gentry of Rustington were few in number, but he believed that they made up for that by their goodness. This might be a pat on the back for themselves, but he would also give their working men one word, he thought they would not find in any village, a better or more honest lot of workmen than they had in this village. Mr Macfarlane then called upon Mrs Wellesley to formally declare the room open. He thanked her for coming amongst them that evening, and he was sure that if Mrs Wellesley's health lasted as long as their good wishes, she would live very many many years."

Mrs Wellesley, who met with an enthusiastic reception, then addressed the company. "It was very kind of them" she said, to ask her to come, and open their reading room, but it was a great pleasure to her, as they knew what an interest her husband and herself took in them. She was exceedingly pleased at the result of their scheme formulated last October. She then declared the room open, wishing its members a long life and every possible success.

A hearty vote of thanks was then proposed to Mrs Wellesley, to which Mr Wellesley suitably responded on behalf of his wife, he concluded by proposing a vote of thanks to Mr Drake for his services. To which that gentleman suitably responded, and the proceedings terminated.

A supper was subsequently partaken of, under the chairmanship of Mr A. Chown, and the remainder of the evening was spent in Toast giving and Harmony. (*The Littlehampton News*, 1893)

THE CRADLE OF THE SUFFRAGE MOVEMENT

This will be something of a surprise to most people when they learn that Rustington was the cradle of the suffrage movement.

The Reverend Stansfield, who lived at The Vicarage, bought a piece of land in the east of The Street and built the large property known as Ffynches Lodge, for his large family, so that they had a home to go to when he retired from the Church, or if he should die.

Millicent Fawcett speaking in Hyde Park in 1913. (12)

Ffynches Lodge was let to Gerald Wellesley's family, who were close relatives of the Duke of Wellington and one of at least two families in the village who were related to royalty (more of this later). Whilst they lived there they became very friendly with other residents of the village, these included Sir Charles Hubert Hastings Parry and Lady Maude Parry (nee Herbert) of Knightscroft House in Sea Lane; Mrs Curtis, who lived opposite to Ffynches Lodge in Walnut Tree House; Sir James Barrie (known as JM Barrie – the creator of Peter Pan) and Arthur Llewelyn Davies (brother of Emily Davies the well-known Suffragist) and his wife Sylvia du Maurier (niece of Daphne du Maurier) along with their sons (they were the inspiration for the Darling family in Peter Pan), who stayed many months each year at Cudlow House, Sea Lane (a former residence of the Parrys); and the Garrett sisters and cousins who rented The Firs (now Old Orchard House) in The Street from 1878-1899 as well as the Urlins who lived at The Grange in Sea Lane.

The Firs (now Old Orchard House), where the Garrett family rented. (13)

It is well known that most of these people were very keen supporters and active members of the suffrage movement. The Garrett sisters played a pivotal role in the development of women's rights. Three of the eleven children of Newson Garrett (1812-1893) and his wife Louisa Dunnell (1813-

1903), from Suffolk, were in Rustington, namely Dame Millicent Garrett (1847-1929) who married the blind postmaster general and Liberal MP (from 1865), Henry Fawcett (PC); Elizabeth Garrett LSA, MD (1836-1917) who married James GS Anderson (a ship owner); and Agnes Garrett (1845-1935) along with their cousin Rhoda Garrett (1841-1882) (the daughter of an impoverished clergyman from Derbyshire whose second wife had practically turned her predecessor's children out of the house to fend for themselves). All of them were to go on to leave their mark in British history.

Photographs of Elizabeth Garrett Anderson (Right: Photo as Mayor of Aldeburgh). (14 &15)

Agnes and her cousin Rhoda went to London in 1867 in search of employment; after a long and fruitless search they managed to apprentice themselves to an architect for three years, which at this time would have been unheard of.

They learnt their trade and soon established themselves as decorators at their house in Gower Street, London. Their interior design firm was the first and only business registered and run by women. Rhoda loved wandering around old churches and other buildings, admiring the noble proportions of architecture and examining the carvings and ancient mouldings and it is believed that she did at one time wish to become an architect. A cottage room exhibited in the Trocadèro at the French Exhibition of 1878 gained very general admiration for its original and simple style; and the Miss Garretts, after long-protracted and patient work attained that success which was so justly their due. They won many high profile commissions for both private residencies and public buildings and one of their first was for Sir Hubert Parry's Kensington home. They were to become great friends. There are a number of pieces of furniture designed by cousins Agnes and Rhoda Garrett on display at the National Trust property Standen. The Parry's home in Rustington also had Garrett furniture and carpets.

Left: Agnes Garrett. (16)

Centre: A mahogany corner cupboard on display at Standen (National Trust Property). (17)

Right: Blue plaque outside 2 Gower Street in London for Millicent Fawcett. (18)

It was Rhoda's delicate health that led her and Agnes to head for Rustington for at least a few months each year.

Agnes's older sister Elizabeth stayed in the village less often (Little Ffynches was her summer house between 1906 and 1912). She was the first British woman to qualify as a physician and surgeon and had the Elizabeth Garrett Anderson Hospital named after her. A gallery has recently been opened at the Unison Centre in Euston Road, London, showing her life and works in the original entrance hall to the hospital. Elizabeth was active in the women's suffrage movement and in 1866, along with Emily Davies, presented more than 1,500 signed petitions to parliament asking for female heads of households to be given the vote. Emily was a great friend of the Garretts and a frequent visitor to Rustington. It was in this year that she joined the first British Women's Suffrage Committee. She then became a member of the Central Committee of the National Society for Women's Suffrage in 1889. Her activities on behalf of the movement increased following her husband's death in 1907 where, as Mayor of Aldeburgh in Suffolk, she gave speeches on behalf of the movement. Elizabeth wrote to Emmeline Pankhurst late in 1911 to tell her that she was withdrawing her membership of the Women's Social and Political Union as the movement had started to increase its militant activities. This was following a letter from Millicent to her sister in December 1911 stating that *"We have the best chance of Women's Suffrage next session that we have ever had, by far, if it is not destroyed by disgusting masses of people by revolutionary violence."* Elizabeth agreed with her sister saying, *"I am quite with you with the WSPU. I think they are quite wrong."* However, Elizabeth's daughter, Louisa Garrett Anderson, who had also joined the WSPU was sent to prison for taking part in the window-breaking campaign. This upset Millicent, she wrote to Elizabeth saying, *"I am in hopes she will take her punishment wisely, that the enforced solitude will help her to see more in focus than she always does."*

Agnes's younger sister Millicent was the most prominent of the sisters in the movement, becoming president of the NUWSS (National Union of Women's Suffrage Societies) from

1897 until 1918, when the vote was secured for women. In 1871 she co-founded Newnham College in Cambridge. Millicent, along with her older sisters Agnes, Elizabeth and their married sister Louise Smith's early interest in the movement and the Liberal Party was increased when attending a speech given in London by John Stuart Mill MP in July 1865.

Right: Millicent Fawcett. (19)

Left: Suffrage Sculpture Scroll in Christchurch Gardens, Victoria Street, London. (20)

Right: Statue of Emmeline Pankhurst outside the Houses of Parliament. (21)

John Stuart Mill became the first person in the history of parliament to call for women to be given the vote in 1866. Although the elder sisters added their names to the petition aforementioned in favour of votes for women, Millicent was considered to be too young. She attended the subsequent debate in May 1867 in which John Stuart Mill vigorously defended his stance for votes for women. Millicent first joined the London Suffrage Committee in 1868; she was an excellent organiser but didn't like speaking in public, she would be so nervous before making speeches that she would be physically ill. As a result she refused to make speeches more than four times a week. Her husband Henry Fawcett's political career at this time was on the rise, so much so that William Gladstone in 1880 appointed him as the Postmaster General and he introduced the parcel post, the sixpenny telegram and postal orders. He also used his leverage as Postmaster General to instigate employment of women medical officers. (Crawford, *The Women's Suffrage Movement in Britain: A Reference Guide 1866-1928*, 1999)

Millicent Garrett and Henry Fawcett on their wedding day. (22)

Millicent also campaigned against the Contagious Diseases Acts, against the trafficking of women and in support of the improvements of conditions for low-paid workers.

As we said earlier, Millicent disapproved of the militant tactics employed by the WSPU, although in her book *What I Remember*, published in 1924, she did say: "*After 1903 the whole country, indeed we might almost say the world, rang with the doings of the Suffragettes, as the violent Suffragists came to be called. I would point out, however, that for at least two years of their activity, 1906-1908, while they suffered extraordinary acts of physical violence, they used none, and all through, from beginning to end of their campaign, they took no life, and shed no blood, either man or beast.*" (Fawcett, 1924). When the British government declared war on Germany on 4th August 1914 the NUWSS declared two days later to suspend all political activity until the war was over, and although Millicent was fervently behind the Great War effort she did not follow the WSPU's strategy of persuading young men to join the armed forces; at this time Emmeline Pankhurst was on the verge of ditching the struggle for women in favour of votes for soldiers in 1917. The Garrett family were to go on to lose twenty-nine members of their extended family during the conflict.

Millicent worked steadfastly and longer than anyone else in the cause for women's suffrage; she had already been campaigning for at least a decade prior to Emmeline Pankhurst joining the Manchester National Society for Women's Suffrage in 1880. Yet, despite all her ministerial lobbying and non-militant action, it was Emmeline Pankhurst who was honoured with a statue outside the Houses of Parliament, and it was Miss Pankhurst's name that entered the public's consciousness, along with Emily Davison jumping in front of the King's horse at the Derby on 4th June 1913, rather than Millicent. This is not really surprising as Millicent never really craved public attention. However, since her death, the Fawcett Library was named after her, which is now called the Women's Library and is housed at the London School of Economics. This houses the library and archives of the Fawcett Society which still campaigns for women's rights.

Agnes and Rhoda, however, in 1867 broke away from the London National Society for Women's Suffrage to which Millicent Fawcett remained loyal, in order to join the executive committee of a new society, the Central Committee of the National Society for Women's Suffrage, a more radical faction. (See Appendix 2 – Letter sent by Agnes Garrett and Caroline Biggs).

Irrational opposition is certain to arise against people of any independence of mind or breadth of view, but Rhoda Garrett was not easily daunted. Therefore, it is no surprise that Rhoda had no fear of being thought strong-minded or unfeminine by becoming an earnest supporter of women's rights, as to this cause of justice she could not help but take an active part. Rhoda became an extremely active speaker in the 1860s-1880s and is pictured many times making speeches.

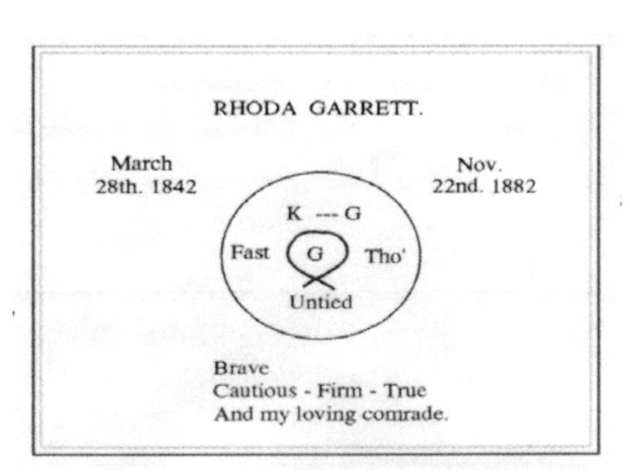

Copy of inscription found at The Old Orchard, formerly The Firs. Unfortunately, no sign of this inscription can be seen today. (23)

Printed afterwards as *Electoral Disabilities of Women*, Rhoda would tour with lectures to show how suffrage could be the first step on the ladder to help the educational, economic and legal position of women. She often protested that the education system prepared boys for life in the world and girls only for life in the home and in the workplace. Rhoda was advocating that proper educational opportunities would arise if women were given the vote; however, others were of the opinion that women would not be ready for voting until they had more education. She stated this in one of her speeches below:

"Would they consent to be excluded from a fair share in educational advantages if they could make their voices heard in the Legislature of the country? Would not their claim to be educated as solidly, and in the same branches of knowledge as men, be argued with a far greater chance of success, if they possessed the power of urging its justice before that tribunal where men are able to lay their grievances, and enforce their redress?"

She also noted that working class women were paid less than their male counterparts even if they were doing the same job, and as for the more educated middle class women there were little or no opportunities to work at all. Parents would never provide the capital for their daughters to set up in business, unlike their sons. So, it is not surprising that most women looked upon marriage as their only course of action.

She also stated in one of her speeches that:

"...We are constantly told, in tones of scorn, that the women who desire the suffrage are a mere handful of female fanatics. As compared with the entire female population we may be only a handful, but we are an ever-increasing handful of very obstinate people."

What a great orator Rhoda was, talking equally well on women's suffrage or interior design. How sad it is that she was unable to see her ideals come to fruition in her short lifetime and it is thanks to Rhoda and Agnes that women owning and running their own businesses is now totally accepted.

Agnes realised that she needed to keep Rustington as a family meeting place after Rhoda's death in 1882, but she was deeply affected by the loss. She wrote to Lady Maud Parry saying:

"I know all she was to me helping me perpetually from sinking into commonplace aims and low ideals. I feel as if I were an ear of wheat that has been threshed and robbed of all the living grains. It is this that has made me shrink so from going on with our work – as if I should have no freshness no originality no delicacy to offer people – in fact that I should be that which she hated so – a charlatan. But no one else seems to think so... I have determined to go on at any rate for the present."

Tragedy was again to hit two years later when Millicent's husband Henry Fawcett died aged 51. Hubert Parry said of Henry that he was the finest and truest man in the whole range of political life. He was to dedicate his funeral ode,

The Glories of our Blood and State, to both Henry and Rhoda. He also said of Millicent that behind the strong and determined exterior she showed to the world lay hidden tenderness and sentiment. Agnes and Millicent became inseparable after this and in 1928, whilst visiting Jerusalem, they danced around the room together when they heard that women were finally being given equal voting rights with men.

Rhoda Garrett addressing the meeting at St. James's Hall, 6th May 1880. (The Graphic 22nd May 1880) (24)

In 1876, she remarked to the audience of the National Association for the Promotion of Social Science, that *"woman's sphere and woman's mission is one of the most important problems of the present day..."* Almost the last act of her life was to write a letter of sympathy to the promoters of the Scottish National Demonstration of Women, which had just been held in Glasgow. Her personality and drive cannot be underestimated enough in the role women have today in all walks of life in this country! This is evident from Lady Maude Parry's reflections on Rhoda's life. She wrote:

"In the world we rarely meet with a truly noble and ideal character. There are many whom we admire for various fine qualities, but a complete human being is a thing so rare that we may live our whole lives through without ever coming across anybody whose humanity impresses us in its very best and widest sense. The world, indeed, is slow to recognise such, and it is only when death has taken them, and we are left in darkness, no longer illuminated by their bright and vivid presence, that we fully realise the immensity of the loss. Those who knew Rhoda Garrett felt, indeed, that she was one of those few and exceptional beings whose personality was strong enough to influence for good all those with whom she came in contact..." and Maude goes on to write about her public speaking, saying, *"With her wide and generous sympathies for mankind in general Rhoda Garrett could not be otherwise than a sincere Radical; and she more especially had at heart the cause of woman's suffrage, and the kindred subjects of women's position and opportunities in the world. Those who heard her speak in public will never forget the impression of that beautiful voice, with its ring of truth and earnestness, carrying conviction as nothing else could; and yet, though burning with genuine enthusiasm, her speeches were as remarkable for their eloquence. A few words from a speech of hers are worth quoting to show her justice and breadth of view on the subject of women's work... This question rests mainly in your own hands. Now the public recognises and, for the most part, it sympathises with your demand to earn your own living. But the public will not pay you for unmarketable commodities. It will not, because you are women, remove all difficulties out of your path. It will, indeed, often hinder you, and often sneer at you; but it cannot stop you, and it will generally deal fairly with you if you show that you know how to do thoroughly what you undertake to do. Let women, then, take advantage of the greater facilities of higher education which are placed within their reach. Let them learn to be thoroughly reasonable and earnest in all the work that they undertake – not blown away by every wind of doctrine, and running hither and thither*

after six things at a time; and then the time will come, I am convinced, when women, as well as men, will be free to choose their own careers – such careers, that is, as are found by experience fit and best for their capabilities and their natures. Ladies, this is my advice to women, and it is based upon experience." Maude then goes on to comment on her speech saying that "*The clearness of expression and well balanced distribution of thought in this passage is sufficient to show that she had unusual readiness in appealing to an audience, and yet no one ever hated speaking more than she did. It was only her enthusiasm for the cause of women and her strong sense of duty that enabled her to pass through such an ordeal."*

Rhoda Garrett addressing a meeting in 1872 with her cousin Millicent Fawcett at the Hannover Square Rooms in London. (25)

Given how delicate, sensitive and sympathetic Rhoda was, it would have been impossible for her to have lived and worked alone but, fortunately, she found in her cousin Agnes one ready to sympathise and able to share in all her labours as we have mentioned earlier.

Pen and ink sketch of Rhoda Garrett and illuminated letter R by Lady Maude Parry. (26 & 27)

Rhoda (left) and Agnes Garrett relaxing in the garden at The Firs. (28)

The Firs (Old Orchard) as it is in 2015. (29)

During Agnes and Rhoda's time in Rustington, other members of the Garrett family would come to stay, including Elsie Garrett (1869-1959), Fydell Edmund Garrett (known as Edmund) (1865-1907), both children of the Rev JF Garrett, and Philippa Garrett Fawcett (1868-1948), the only daughter of Henry and Millicent Fawcett.

Elsie Garrett also lived at The Firs prior to her marriage at East Preston Church to Charles Emmanuel Rice. She became a botanical artist in South Africa. Her grandson was the actor Sir Nigel Hawthorne.

Philippa was educated at Newnham College, Cambridge and in 1890 became the first woman to come top in the Cambridge Mathematical Tripos exams, receiving 13% more marks than the next highest. However, she did not receive the title of senior wrangler as only men were allowed this title. Coming amidst the women's suffrage movement the result gathered huge international coverage. The lead story in *The Telegraph* the following day said, *"Once again has woman demonstrated her superiority in the face of incredulous and unsympathetic world... And now the trench has been carried by Amazonian assault, and the whole citadel of learning lies open and defenceless before the victorious students of Newnham and Girton. There is no longer any field of learning in which the lady student does not excel."*

Philippa was to later set up with her mother the educational system in the Transvaal following the Boer War. Millicent had been asked, by the British government in August 1901, to head a committee of British women to investigate Emily Hobhouse's (a member of the NUWSS) complaints about the conditions in the concentration camps in South Africa during the Anglo-Boer War. The Fawcett Commission reported that 27,927 Boers had died of starvation, disease and exposure in the concentration camps, following Kitchener's 'Scorched Earth' policy which involved the destruction of crops, the slaughtering of livestock, the poisoning of wells, salting of fields and the systematic burning of homesteads and livestock. Civilians were then moved by force to the concentration camps. The report said that about a quarter of all Boer inmates, mostly children, had died.

Edmund Garrett was the half-brother of Rhoda. He was brought up by Agnes, Millicent and Rhoda, until Millicent's marriage when he became Agnes's special charge following the death of Rhoda whilst he was at a public school. He was 'her boy' and she to him throughout his life, was 'mother, sister, friend'. Edmund was to go on to have an eminent career as a journalist, a great friend of Cecil Rhodes; he went on to live in South Africa for many years following being diagnosed with tuberculosis.

Edmund would spend most of his holidays at his favourite home from his childhood, The Firs, with Rhoda and Agnes of which he wrote in his memoirs. *"I live,"* he wrote, *"with many memories of old Rustington days – the old cottage; you; Rhoda; my boyish tiresomeness and worshippings; the corner in the churchyard; the seat just the other side of the kitchen-garden wall; the picnic breakwater; the moonlight walks; a hundred old pages."* One great delight of the holidays was the sea-bathing, under the tutelage at first of Sir Hubert Parry; another was the decoration of a railway carriage, which had been bought as a play room for him and his cousin, Miss Philippa Fawcett. 'The Ark', they called it and it was decorated by them with famous frescoes of the deluge. It was to be Edmund's lot to live much abroad and in an English colony, and he became a devoted lover of the Greater Britain. But no roses were ever so sweet to him as those that bloomed at Rustington, and even the delight of the sea at Muizenburg owed something of its pleasure to memories of the surf in which he had bathed during long summer days at home.

Left: Fydell Edmund Garrett. (30)

Right: *Philippa Garrett Fawcett. (31)*

When Agnes and Rhoda Garrett set up their home at The Firs, their friend, the composer Dame Ethel Smyth DBE (1858-1944) (who had been introduced to the family by Barbara Hamlet, a mutual friend) came to live with them. In her book, *Impressions that Remained* (1919), she wrote about her time in the village and the Garrett family. Dame Ethel Smyth said of the village that *"Rustington was then quite an unfrequented spot a few straggling old cottages and farmhouses, a fine Norman Church, sometimes flicked by spray when south-west gales blew, and an almost deserted*

beach." She also added that *"The beach at Rustington is connected in my mind with one of the oddest manifestations of the tender passion I ever heard of. A certain man we knew, not a bachelor, was secretly beloved only it wasn't quite a secret by a maiden of gentle birth. The man, a strong swimmer, was in the habit of seeking out desolate places on the shore, depositing his garments in a bundle among the brush-wood, and swimming out miles and miles to sea. One day when he returned he found a little bunch of flowers and thought it was a joke of some passing stranger... but next day the same thing happened. Much perturbed, he varies his jumping-off place, but without success, for the hour of high tide is no secret and he was marked down by this infatuated maiden again and again. Just as I was leaving Rustington his much amused wife told us he talked of giving up bathing."*

In her time in Rustington, Dame Ethel Smyth was totally indifferent to the suffragette cause. However, this changed when she met and fell in love with Emmeline Pankhurst (the founder of the Women's Social and Political Union) in 1910. The following year she composed the WSPU battle song, *The March of the Women.* In 1912, as part of the WSPU's new campaign of large scale smashing of shop windows, both Emmeline Pankhurst and Ethel Smyth were arrested and sent to Holloway Prison. Ethel had smashed the window of an anti-suffrage politician in Downing Street. She spent two months inside Holloway.

The Garretts were also very friendly with the vicar's family, especially Alice Stansfield, one of the reverend's daughters. They would often spend time together either at The Vicarage, The Firs or at the Parry's house. We have seen many entries in both Hubert Parry's and Maude's diaries alluding to this, along with letters from Agnes and Rhoda to and from Maude at this time, especially at times when illness fell upon either Hubert or Maude. Both Agnes and Rhoda were very protective of their friends.

The death of Rhoda on 22nd November 1882, from typhoid fever and bronchitis, at 2 Gower Street, London, was to greatly affect her family and close friends. Her cousin Elizabeth Garrett Anderson was to fittingly sign the death certificate and she was buried, in the little churchyard where she had herself expressed a wish to rest, at Rustington. It is quite incredible to believe that there is no trace of this remarkable lady's grave to be seen today in the churchyard; a great many of the older gravestones have been removed over the years without respect for whom some of these people were and perhaps even because women at this time were still classed as second class citizens! Agnes did not want to leave The Firs and go back to London following her cousin's death, but after a while she realised that The Firs was too large for her on her own, so she rented a cottage nearly opposite, called Pound Cottage, between the years 1899-1905. She then returned to live with her widowed sister, Millicent, and her niece, Philippa, at 2 Gower Street until her death in 1935, aged 90. The Garrett connection with 2 Gower Street continued until 1938 when, three years after Agnes's death, Philippa gave up the tenancy. (Crawford, *Enterprising Women: The Garretts and their Circle*, 2002)

To see how much Rhoda's death meant we have extracted three quotes from some of the people she knew best. Firstly, we have extracted parts of Sir Hubert Parry's diary from November 1882 as follows:

23rd November 1882

Wild and wet most of the day. Maude came back before lunch... In the evening after dinner I was playing when she walked in with a fired expression on her face & said something which I did not catch, & handed me a post card from Alice Stansfield, on which were written only the cruel words "No more Hope" Wednesday night. She was my food and brain, but unnaturally quiet, & still both hope that better news may come tomorrow. The last card said poor Rhoda has been very bad however, & the terrible disaster seems almost certain.

24th November 1882

Met the postman in the morning and he handed me a note from Agnes telling me that the blow had fallen, and dear Rhoda had died yesterday. Even in her desolation Agnes thought for Maude, & wanted me with a kindness for her so that I might tell her in the best way to avoid a shock. Maude took it very well, but gradually succumbed under it. Alice Stansfield came later in the day, looking haggard and agonized. Maude and her spent much time together, & I thought best to leave them alone, but they must have been taken with much weepings before their spirits could approach any sort of quietude again. It was a terrible day.

25th November 1882

Most of the morning spent in getting flowers for Rhoda's coffin poor Alice came again. The funeral was in the afternoon. The sight of those good women Agnes & Mrs Fawcett & Miss Williamson was perfectly agonizing. Agnes was wonderfully calm, but white and angelic looking. Something supernatural. They were all wonderfully restrained; but Mr Stansfield had to make a long stop in reading the kind service & his voice faltered and I had the greatest difficulty in holding myself. I felt on the verge of a veritable explosion. Maude helped me out strangely enough. I think this wonderful collectedness struck me as something so very terrible that it altogether beat me. I looked down into the deep grave and thus a few last flowers and then took Maude home. She went after to see Agnes and I waited for her outside...

26th November 1882

In the morning Maude out to see Alice again, & I took a little walk in my sad humour after leaving her at the vicarage, hard looking at the grave which is prettily covered with wreaths and bunches of flowers. In the afternoon I waited while Maude was at church to take her on to the Firs after, & later Agnes came in the dark and I played her some Bach; the last chorus of the Passion, which she specially wished for, and Chorales & the 2 major Fugues next. She was my calm and quiet. Altogether the saddest sight to see. Her strength and being, & even brightness seem to throw her desolateness, & the breakdown of that beautiful connection between them into stronger relief. It is most piteous. Maude was much lighter on the whole today...

27th November 1882

...Agnes came later and I played a lot of quiet things to her. She keeps marvellously bright...

28th November 1882

Fine but cold. N.W. wind. Directly after breakfast with Maude to say goodbye to Agnes Garrett at the Cottage. It was very sad and it seemed the last farewell to all the happy feelings which centre round that sweet little corner.

Secondly, a letter dated Friday December 1st 1882, in reply to a letter written by Lady Maude Parry by the then 17-year-old Edmund Garrett (Rhoda's half-brother):

My dear Lady Maud,

Thank you very much for taking the trouble to write to me, for I like to hear what people think and feel about Rhoda, though I can't say much about it myself. I can hardly understand what has happened – hardly realize that thousands of words, phrases, conversations & sayings, looks and deeds, and all the things that I remember so well, are now nothing more than a memory. It seems to me very hard. What you say is exactly true. She was different from everyone else. Others might be good, others unselfish, others kind, others earnest, but there never was another Rhoda, there is only one, and I think there never will be another. That shows her genius; but the myriad of things that show her perseverance & hard work & unselfishness are to me the most comforting and valuable. We are born with talents; and if we have genius, it is ours from birth; I can see little to love in it, however much we admire; it is steadfast earnest use of abilities that strikes me most; it seems so unattainable, so much above. Rhoda was one among a thousand in her wonderful charm and influence & genius but she was one among a million in the use she made of these; – I hardly know yet what a hole her loss has made in my life. She had such a Purpose about my life, that I believe she would have given half her own to see me with the power – which I never possessed – of acting so as to fulfil it. You say truly, indeed, that she made as all perfect, in the sense that without her we feel as if we had lost the better half of ourselves. As for Belief, – I only know that what St James says of it, – that 'the devils also believe – and shudder!' has a deeper meaning to my mind than was ever meant, I think – judge her by her fruits, – and to every 'good' 'respectable' 'pious' churchgoer that 'pities' her, I give the lie, and I say they may thank their God if they are worthy to touch the hem of her garment! I do not know about meeting again, I do not think I am up to that level; but I do think, that if the very memory alone of all the happiness she has wrought for others is not making her happy herself, there is no justice in heaven or earth! Thank you for your real & valuable sympathy: – I think she lives in Agnes, – and I her deeds. The actions of the just smell sweet and blossom in their dust.

Yours gratefully... Edmund Garrett."

And finally, Dame Ethel Smyth in her book *Impressions that Remained* (1919), written about her time in the village and the Garrett family, saying:

"*One day in November... a telegram was put into my hand. Rhoda had not written for a week and Agnes had let me know she was rather ill; this message told me she was dead... Italy slipped away from me and for many weeks I only saw Rustington. There are few spots on earth, I imagine, of which anyone can say: 'There, at least I was perfectly happy' but whenever the beach at Rustington suddenly stands before my mind's eye, that thought swims up with the vision... I am glad to think of her lying within the shadow of the old church, close to the stretch of sea we both loved better than any other..."*

Dame Ethel went on to reminisce further, saying:

"Late in the autumn of 1880 Barbara introduced me to these great friends of her, and during the next two years their house became the focus of my English life owing to the friendship that sprang up between Rhoda and me.

Both women were a good deal older than I, how much I never knew – nor wished to know, for Rhoda and I agreed that age and income are relative things concerning which statistics are tiresome and misleading. How shall one describe that magic personality of hers, at once elusive and clear cut, shy and audacious? – A dark cloud with a burning heart – something that smoulders in repose and bursts into flame at a touch... Though the most alive, amusing, and amused of people, to me at least the sombre background was always there – perhaps because the shell was so obviously too frail for the spirit. One knew of the terrible struggle in the past to support herself and the young brothers and sisters; that she had been dogged by ill-health as well as poverty – heroic, unflinching through all. Agnes once said to me, 'Rhoda has had more pain in her life than was good for her,' but no one guessed that like her brother Edmund – champion of Rhodes, youthful collaborator with Lord Milner, cut off at the zenith of his powers – she carried in her the seeds of tubercular disease. And yet when the end came there was little of surprise in one's grief; thus again and again had one seen falling stars burn out.

I spoke of her humour; on the whole I think she was more amusing than anyone I have ever met – a wit half scornful, always surprising, as unlike everyone else's as was her person ...a slim, lithe being, very dark, with deep-set burning eyes that I once made her laugh by saying reminded me of a cat in a coal scuttle. Yet cat's eyes are never tender, and hers could be the tenderest in the world.

I always think the feel of a hand as it grasps yours is a determining factor in human relationships, and all her friends must well remember Rhoda's – the soft skin that only dark people have, the firm, wiry, delicate fingers. My reason tells me she was almost plain, but one looked at no one else when she was in a room. There was an enigmatic quality in her witchery behind which the grand lines, the purity and nobility of her soul, stood out like the bone in some enchanted landscape. No one had a subtle hold on the imagination of her friends, and when she died it was as if laughter, astonishment, warmth, light, mystery, had been cut off at the source. The beauty of the relation between the cousins, and of that home life in Gower Street, remains with us who knew them as certain musical phrases haunt the melomaniac, and but for Agnes, who stood as far as possible between her and the slings and arrows which are the reward of pioneers, no doubt Rhoda's life would have been spent much earlier. Her every burden, human and otherwise, was shouldered by Agnes, and both had a way of discovering waifs and strays of art more or less worsted by life whose sanctuary their house henceforth became.

I think I have never been happier in my life than at the old thatched cottage they rented at Rustington. An exhausting fight against the stream of prejudice, such as the Garretts had waged for many years, was not to be my portion till later. Of course both cousins and all their friends were ardent Suffragists, and I wonder now at the patience with which they supported my total indifference on the subject – an indifference I was to make up for thirty years later.

Their great friends the Parrys had a house close by, and besides helping me with the invaluable musical criticism and advice Hubert Parry lent me a canoe, in which on very calm days, cautiously dressed in bathing costume, I put to sea. There too I got to know the Fawcetts, and saw how that living monument of courage, the blind Postmaster General, impressed the country people as he strode up and down hills in the company of his wife. I thought Mrs Fawcett rather cold, but an incident that happened the summer after the death of Rhoda, to whom she was devoted, taught me otherwise. One day when I was singing an Irish melody I had often sung at Rustington – 'At the Mid Hour of Night' – I suddenly noticed that tears were rolling down her cheeks, and presently she got up and quietly left the room. After that for many years I never saw her. Then came the acute Suffrage struggle, during which the gulf that separated Militants from National Unionists belched forth flames, but through all those years, remembering that incident, I always thought of Mrs Fawcett with affection." (Smythe, 1919)

Millicent Garrett (with book) and Agnes Garrett c. 1865. (32)

Following the death of Rhoda, Agnes used to accompany Millicent Fawcett everywhere during the years of the suffrage campaign. One of the places they would go was a summer cottage, as guests of their sister Dr Elizabeth Garrett Anderson, in a beautiful part of the Highlands at Newtonmore in Inverness-shire.

One of the Garrett brothers summed up Elizabeth Garrett Anderson one day, as of being a younger woman at heart than age, by saying that contrary to everybody's entreaties and advice, she insisted on clambering down a steep incline under the unshakable impression that it was a short cut home. *"You must make allowances, I suppose, for her being the first woman doctor,"* he observed, when she had had time to realise her error and he was setting off to fetch her back. Undoubtedly, like Florence Nightingale and other reformers who have had to fight both prejudice and vested interests, if Elizabeth Garrett Anderson had been the sweetly reasonable person who always believes what she is told without questioning it, she would not have been the pioneer who opened the medical profession to women. The author and suffragist Evelyn Sharp also stayed with her on a few occasions. For those involved with the preoccupations of the struggle of woman's suffrage over many years appreciated a week or two away from the campaign up in the peace and tranquillity of the Highlands. Evelyn Sharp said of Elizabeth that in her own home she was a most hospitable and lovable hostess, and had a delicious sense of humour, which may have been one reason why she was instantly attracted towards the militant branch of the suffrage movement when it became prominent. Her daughter, Dr Louisa Garrett Anderson, who brought the same gifts of courage and perception, so rare in combination, to the service of the same cause, inherited all her mother's brains and culture, and more than her personal charm and gentleness. On one or two occasions peace was invaded when both Millicent Fawcett and Emmeline Pankhurst came to stay whilst in the course of conducting speaking tours. Evelyn Sharp remarked that it was quite entertaining to meet both these famous characters in the more intimate and human surroundings of a summer holiday and couldn't grudge the time given to working up a suffrage meeting in the village instead of tramping about the hills. (Sharp, 1933)

We know that the families involved with the suffrage movement in Rustington would often meet at each other's homes; it would seem most often at Ffynches Lodge, with the Wellesleys. Sometimes at Cudlow House where Thomas Hardy amongst others was a visitor and parties and picnics were held at The Firs.

Friends and colleagues of these people, mostly suffragettes who lived in and around London, came down to visit and would stay at what was once called Roland House in East Street, Littlehampton. However, at this time it was called The Green Lady Hostel (This is now called Mewsbrook House and is a nursing/care home). The locals still call the footpath that runs between East Street and Cornwall Road the 'The Green Lady'.

(33)

The property was purchased by Lily Montagu CBE and Mrs Emmeline Pethick-Lawrence as a seaside holiday house for female factory workers and established by Mary Neal and Emmeline (founders of the Espèrence Girls' Club) in 1900.

It was known as The Green Lady Hostel as at this time the majority of suffragettes took it upon themselves to wear green suits and white blouses, or green dresses. Special jewellery was designed for them to wear, in particular emeralds and seed pearls set in gold. These items today are very highly sought after.

(34)

The former Green Lady Hostel in 2015 with the blue plaque on the wall pictured right, along the path known as 'The Green Lady'. (35)

Lady Maude Parry, who had a very strong character, and as we have seen was a very eloquent writer, and her husband (Sir Hubert) were very much behind the suffrage movement in their own right. Often attending marches Lady Maude would chair suffrage meetings including one held at The Lecture Hall in Littlehampton where Millicent Fawcett (Mrs Henry Fawcett as it was advertised) the then president of the NUWSS was to give an address.

Lady Maude Parry leading suffragist marches in 1913. (36 & 37)

When Sir Hubert Parry wrote the music to *Jerusalem* in March 1916, he had doubts about the music being put to the words of William Blake's poem for use in the Fight for

Right campaign. He withdrew support for the song being used in the campaign entirely in May 1917. It was then taken up by the suffragettes in 1917. His long-time friend Millicent Fawcett asked Parry if she could use it at the Suffrage Demonstration Concert on 13th March 1918; he was delighted and he orchestrated the piece (it had originally been for the organ and vocals).

Sir Hubert Parry. (38)

Not long after, Millicent wrote to Parry asking him if it could become the *Women Voters' Hymn.*

He replied to her saying, *"I wish indeed it might become the Women Voters' Hymn, as you suggest. People seem to enjoy singing it. And having the vote ought to diffuse a good deal of joy. So they should combine happily."*

In the April 1918 *Scribble Magazine* there were two columns devoted to women's suffrage. The first, written by the editor of the magazine, shows some amazing chauvinism (although it could have been said in jest), but it does show the strength of feeling at this time and what the Garretts and others had to put up with. The first column is as follows:

In another column of this issue we refer to the meeting at Littlehampton on April 12th. It was indeed a pleasure to listen to Mrs. Henry (Millicent) Fawcett, and Lady Maud Parry made an excellent Chairwoman, although it might have been better if she had insisted on a time limit.

Sir Hubert gave us about an hour of most interesting

reminiscences, ranging from ladies' hats to mustard plasters, with a little sea bathing thrown in.

Three questions to Mrs Fawcett elicited the following facts, that:

1. *Suffragettes intend to become members of Parliament.*
2. *They do not at present intend to run independent candidates.*
3. *When women have equal voting powers with men they will have a large majority of votes.*

Unless, therefore, we follow the Chinese system with girl babies, the House of Commons in years to come will be run by women.

If this should happen, we anticipate that Westminster Abbey will have to be given over to Members' babies and their nurses. Specials would then indeed be necessary to regulate the perambulator traffic.

We certainly believe, as has been proved, that women can do a lot to help government of the country both in parochial and parliamentary affairs, but when it comes to having unequal voting powers of the country behind them which can enforce 'petticoat government', man would then become a 'mere thing'. As, in the beginning, women was sent into the world to be a 'helpmeet' to man, and it is told to us in Genesis that man should rule over woman, they will never be able to exercise their voting powers to carry all before them. (Hollis, 1918)

The other is a more serious article and is as follows:

It should be of interest to readers of Scribble to learn that Mrs Henry Fawcett, President of the National Union of Women's Suffrage, in commemoration of the passing of the Women's Suffrage Bill, was chief speaker on April 12th at Littlehampton. Mrs Fawcett was supported by Sir C. Hubert H Parry, Bart., Lady Maud Parry being in the chair. That the president of the N.U.W.S. should consent to speak in this locality, after refusing over 100 requests to speak elsewhere, is both a compliment to her local supporters and also a token of the memory of old ties with Rustington, where as long ago as 40 years, she and her husband the late Postmaster-General, were wont to stay, and where, with a small coterie of relations and friends, women's suffrage was discussed, and a petition for it was signed by a large proportion of Rustington people. It has been said that Rustington was the cradle of women's suffrage.

An anti-militant, Mrs Fawcett has worked with dignity, fidelity, and an infinite patience for the cause which has been for so long the ambition of thousands of thinking men and women.

The lecture hall was filled with an enthusiastic audience, and an interesting message was received from Sir Harry Johnson, who regretted his inability to be present, but who said that he was only just recovering from a 'whiff' of mustard gas inhaled near the German lines. "We look now". He said, "to the men and women of the masses to save this country and all the best things that this great Empire stands for, to save us from mismanagement of the educated upper classes, and to save us from the general effects all round of a most inadequate education in all things that really matter. To save us from the waste and plunder that has hitherto characterised our methods of government." We have referred to other items, less serious, in our editorial. (Hollis, *Women's Suffrage*, 1918)

Prior to his death, Sir Hubert Parry on 7th October 1918 assigned the copyright of *Jerusalem* to the NUWSS. where it remained until the society's winding up in 1928. His executors then reassigned the copyright to the Women's Institutes up until 1968 when it was to go into the public domain.

In the end it was Millicent Fawcett who was instrumental in gaining the vote for six million British women over the age of 30 in 1918. (A memorial inscription was added to the monument to Henry Fawcett in 1932 by Sir Herbert Baker which reads "*Dame Millicent Garrett 1847-1929 – A wise constant and courageous Englishwoman. She won citizenship for Women.*")

Extract from Parry's original manuscript of Jerusalem (1916). (39)

Order of Service for Millicent Fawcett's memorial. (40)

WESTMINSTER ABBEY.

Unveiling of the Memorial

to

DAME MILLICENT GARRETT FAWCETT

SATURDAY, 12th MARCH, 1932

12 noon.

Order of Service.

The General Thanksgiving, with special commemoration of Dame Millicent Fawcett.

The Dean will then invite Viscount Cecil of Chelwood to unveil the Memorial and to give an Address.

Which done, the prayers following will be said:

Let us pray.

Lord, have mercy upon us.

Christ, have mercy upon us.

Lord, have mercy upon us.

Our Father . . . . deliver us from evil.—Amen.

O ETERNAL Lord God, who holdest all souls in life: We beseech thee to shed forth upon thy whole Church in Paradise and on earth the bright beams of thy light and heavenly comfort; and grant that we, following the good example of those who have loved and served thee here and are now at rest, may at the last enter into the fulness of thine unending joy; through Jesus Christ our Lord.—*Amen.*

ETERNAL GOD, in whom the spirits of just men do rest in peace from their labours; we bless and praise Thy holy Name for all Thy servants who, having fought a good fight, have finished their earthly course; and we beseech Thee give us grace so to follow their good examples, that here we may be united to them in fellowship of spirit and hereafter we may be gathered together with them in the glory of Thy heavenly presence, through Jesus Christ our Lord.—*Amen.*

THE BLESSING.

Memorial monument at Westminster Abbey. (41)

THE PARRY FAMILY

Charles Hubert Hastings Parry was born on 27th February 1848 in Bournemouth, being the second son of Thomas Gambier Parry, a well-to-do man who achieved considerable reputation as a highly skilled amateur painter and designer, patron of the arts, author of books on art and other subjects. Among his works was the nave ceiling in Ely Cathedral, which he designed and painted, as well as the murals in Highnam Church the building whereof he financed. Tragically, his mother died just twelve days after he was born, and this was the first of several shadows that clouded his life.

His father re-married, and Hubert spent his early childhood divided between Bournemouth and Highnam Court (a few miles west of Gloucester). He is said to have begun composing music at school at the age of eight, at this time hymn tunes and chants. His great enthusiasm for music increased after hearing the great organist Samuel Sebastian Wesley whilst at school in Twyford. In 1861 Hubert Parry, now aged 13, went to Eton, where he spent a good deal of his time at his music, becoming quite famous among his peers for his singing (he had an excellent baritone voice), playing the piano and composing.

Further shadows appeared in his life during his period at Eton. He had to live down the outrageous behaviour of his elder brother Clinton at Oxford, where he was sent down for womanising, drinking and taking opium. His sister Lucy died of consumption (TB) in 1861. Nevertheless, Hubert studied hard and went on to become the youngest person ever to successfully sit the Oxford Bachelor of Music whilst still at Eton in 1867.

He went on to do a BA degree in Law and Modern History at Exeter College, Oxford, where his music started to get slightly neglected. During the long holidays from university

Parry spent several vacations in Germany, learning the language, studying opera, playing the piano and viola. We understand the German influence shows in some of his early works.

Another shadow to hang over Parry's life was Joseph Joachim, the eminent Hungarian violinist, conductor, composer and teacher, who in the role of critic led him to shelve his music on more than one occasion; for example his *Nonet for Wind in Four Movements* he forgot about altogether.

After leaving university, he went into business as an underwriter at Lloyd's of London, but after only a short while he decided city life was not for him. So he left Lloyd's and devoted himself to the art he loved.

Parry had a childhood sweetheart, Lady Elizabeth Maud Herbert. (The spelling of Maud here is as per her birth certificate. However, she and all her friends and acquaintances would use either Maud or Maude, usually the latter, so we shall use both as well.) Lady Maud's mother was extremely worried about their relationship and the possibility of them getting married, for she could see that Parry's first love was his music. Her apprehension caused her to write a thirteen page letter to Parry, urging him not to marry her daughter, another point being they were not of the same class. Parry was not of the aristocracy while Maud was, she being the sister of the 14th Earl of Pembroke. However, despite everything, at the age of 25, Parry married his Maud in 1872.

Hubert Parry was about 28 years old when he first came to West Sussex on account of his wife's poor health. Littlehampton had been recommended as a suitable and quiet place for a rest and a change, so on 12th June 1876 the Parrys came down to stay by the sea. Littlehampton proved to be a great success as Lady Maud recovered much of her strength. It is reported that he said, *"I never saw any place suit her so well."*

Parry took a liking to the area as well, he particularly liked the sea, sculling the River Arun up to the Black Rabbit and beyond and enjoying some very long walks. He would often make friends with children playing on the beach, having great fun paddling, shrimping, building sandcastles for them and what he called 'very small cricket'. Unfortunately, acts as innocent as they were then are frowned upon now.

There was one fly in the ointment however, this being the hotel life. He hated it. The landlady, who ran this hotel, expressed the hope on their second visit that he would not play the piano-forte as much as before! So after only a couple of weeks in 1877, of what he called 'miserable, dependent, disturbed hotel life', they moved into a small place in South Terrace, where he was able to have at least privacy, and his piano.

It was also now that the close association with the sea began. The changeable moods and the tempestuous violence of the sea absolutely fascinated him. He writes in his diary that *"the sight of the stormy waves at night only lit by stars, made him feel inclined to shout with delight."* He also took great pleasure in watching the waves by day from the long narrow pier by the river and thought it most exhilarating to see the waves bubbling and hissing all around him. He also bathed and swam in all weathers, and was never more pleased than when he was tossed about in the water like a cork.

On the Parrys' third season in Littlehampton, Hubert thought nothing of taking himself on some twenty to thirty mile walks around the area, one of his favourite treks being to Arundel and Lyminster water meadows. But his main object in 1878 was to go house hunting. An eligible house situated in Rustington was snapped up under their very noses, but at long last a suitable house was found and rented in Rustington, this being Cudlow House in Sea Lane. They had moved into it by the middle of July 1878.

Sadly the Parrys did not have a son to carry on the name,

but had the great happiness of two lovely daughters, Dorothea (Dolly), born in 1876, and Gwendoline, born in 1878. Now, being a family man, he wanted his own home in the village he had come to love. True, his roots were in Highnam, but 'dear little Rusty' (as he called the village) was his very own, so he started negotiations to buy some land and by the summer of 1880 the workmen had started to build Knights Croft, his elder daughter Dolly, aged four, being given the honour of laying the first brick on 16th August, 1880. Progress on the house was slow, it being hampered by the great gale of November 1880 which nearly blew it all down. After getting going again, work was held up once more in January 1881 by the heavy snowstorms. However, despite all of this, the family were finally able to move into their new home, Knights Croft, on 22nd July, 1881. The workmen, some forty-six in all, were given a feast with plenty of liquid refreshment, followed by games, and most of them moved off on the following day.

Sir Hubert and Lady Maud outside Knightscroft House. (42)

He planted out the gardens with trees, shrubs, lawns and flowers, a particular favourite of his being white violets, which grew there in abundance. Strangely, he very often used the little white violets as a button-hole, as can be seen in several photographs of him.

Whenever time could be found he involved himself with village life, helping with a magic lantern show in the school, giving a Dickens reading, supporting the village cricket club and lecturing on astronomy, a favourite study.

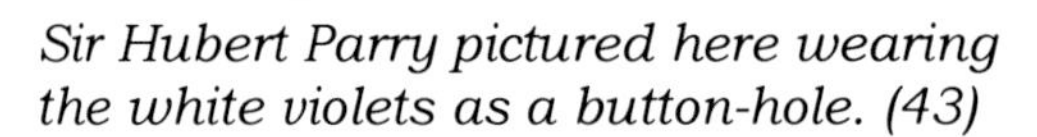

Sir Hubert Parry pictured here wearing the white violets as a button-hole. (43)

As we have seen from Maud's pen and ink sketch of Rhoda Garrett, she was an excellent artist and was involved in the suffrage movement. Hubert Parry wrote in his journal that having the Garretts in the village kept Maud in wonderful good spirits and she was devoted to them. It was often remarked how handsome Lady Maud and her daughters Gwen and Dolly were, perhaps from Maud's Russian paternal grandmother, the Countess Ekaterina Woronzow. (She was the daughter of the Russian Ambassador for Britain from 1785.) Woronzow Road in St. John's Wood, London is named after the family.

We have already stated that Maud was a member of the aristocracy, namely the Herbert, Spencer and Churchill families. In fact, following detailed research by Graeme into her family tree, we found that she was the 4th cousin (four times removed) of Prince William, Duke of Cambridge. (Maud's 3 times great-grandfather and the Duke's 7 times great-grandfather on his mother's side was Charles

Spencer, 3rd Earl of Sunderland from Althorp, Northamptonshire who married Lady Anne Churchill.) She was also the 3rd cousin twice removed of Sir Winston Churchill, and her daughter Gwen's grandson's wife is the designer Mary Quant, famous for designing the mini-skirt in the 1960s. (See partial family tree in appendices.)

Maud's father was Sidney Herbert, 1st Baron of Lea (PC) and a Conservative MP. He was responsible for the War Office during the Crimean War. It was he who sent his friend Florence Nightingale out to Scutari and with Nightingale led the movement for army health and War Office reform after the war. His statue can be seen today next to Florence Nightingale's in Waterloo Place, adjacent to the Crimean Monument.

In 1884, a small yacht, *Ornis*, was built for Parry by Harveys of Littlehampton. This was the first of his fleet; other yachts were the *Hoopee*, *Dolgwandle* and later the *Wanderer*. He often went out to sea regardless of the weather and more than once had a severe ducking and was lucky to get back.

It would seem on consideration that these walks, the sea, yachting and the village life in Rustington, were his total relaxation from his musical world in London and Oxford.

In 1885, he developed heart trouble. During one of his lectures to the students at the Royal College of Music, he almost totally collapsed and his doctors ordered a long holiday. So he took most of the year of 1886 off, to explore the length and breadth of South America. He went without his wife. On his return, he was given a hero's welcome by his students.

In 1887, the year of Queen Victoria's Golden Jubilee, Hubert Parry became nationally famous for his composition *Blest Pair of Sirens*. This was recently sung by the choirs of Westminster Abbey and the Chapel Royal at the wedding of the Duke and Duchess of Cambridge on 29th April 2011.

Several other lesser known compositions of Parry's were also performed at the wedding. (One wonders when selecting this anthem for their wedding if the Duke realised that he was related to the composer!)

Sir Hubert Parry on his boat 'Wanderer'. (44)

In 1888 he wrote the hymn tune *Repton*, the tune that is used now for the popular hymn *Dear Lord and Father of Mankind.*

Over the next few years his musical work increased, including the hymn tune named *Rustington.* Graeme sang the words of *Through the Night of Doubt and Sorrow* to this tune when he was in the Rustington Church Choir.

Parry's feelings for the countryside hereabouts is shown in the way he immortalised local villages by naming hymn tunes after places that so enchanted him: *Amberley*, *Angmering* and *Storrington.*

During the 1890s, Dolly and Gwen were in their teenage years, they were intelligent and full of character, like their parents. Gwen was tall even at the age of 12. She was a wonderful fiddle player for a child. However, Dolly, who was a more delicate girl, had even more of a musical gift as well as acting and writing plays. At this time she wished to go on the stage. Like her mother and father, Dolly was to keep very informative diaries.

Sir Hubert Parry and Lady Maude at Knightscroft House. (45)

There is one lovely story about Sir Hubert Parry we feel we must share with you: While he was away from Knightscroft at any time, one of the maids would seize the opportunity of playing his piano. One day the inevitable happened, for he returned unexpectedly, and she, unaware of this carried on playing. He, instead of issuing a reprimand, came and sat beside her and taught her how the piece should be played. This, it seems, was typical of the man, he liked genuine people and hated shams. He believed in musicians being well educated in other spheres, to be broadminded, thinking men and women.

He was appointed Director of the Royal College of Music. In

1898, Queen Victoria made Parry a Knight, and the same year his elder daughter, Dolly, married Arthur Ponsonby, son of Sir Henry Ponsonby, secretary to the Queen.

In 1899, Gwen was married to Plunket Greene the Irish baritone singer. Parry wrote as a Christmas present to his son-in-law *When comes my Gwen*, number 1 of 6 of his *English Lyrics.*

Under the date June 21st 1902, in Parry's diary, we read: *"Had a letter from Lord Salisbury in the morning, saying His Majesty King Edward VII proposed to make me a Baronet."* Three days later, June 24th, he attended the rehearsal of the Coronation, and there heard that the King was undergoing an operation, and the Coronation, due to take place on the 26th, was to be postponed.

Parry had written the anthem *I was Glad* for the Coronation procession into Westminster Abbey. It is a composition full of fervour and pageantry and it is little wonder that our Queen chose the same anthem for her processional hymn in 1953. However, getting back to King Edward VII's Coronation, it eventually took place on Saturday August 9th 1902. Another quote from Parry's diary from 9th August: *"On this day up early and got into my levee clothes. The Brougham arrived at 8a.m. We were delayed on the road by troops, had to get out and walk a good way to the Abbey – Didn't get away from Abbey past 3p.m. Back to 17,* [Kensington Square, his London residence] *hastily packed and down to Victoria – great crowds everywhere – Train to Arundel, arrived about 7p.m. and found Maud there to meet me, drove together to Rusty."*

Looking back at one of Sir Hubert Parry's diary entries, we noticed that it was JM Barrie who got him hooked on driving. On February 27th 1904, his 56th birthday, he wrote: *"In the afternoon Mr & Mrs Barrie came for me in a motor and whirled me around Regents Park and back in no time. Very amusing experience, and interesting to see how quickly responsive the steering gear is in the crowded streets."*

On 4th September 1904 he wrote: *"Took my first turn at driving the motor car after tea, and found it decidedly difficult."* He obviously didn't find it difficult for very long as we read later of him driving about all over the country. One account states: He drove down the steep and winding road which leads from Savernake Forest into Marlborough at such a pace, that when they reached the bottom, the chauffeur got out and was sick! So this insight into his life would have to include a courtroom scene as follows: The composer is standing nervously in the dock as the presiding magistrate delivers his judgement: *"Sir Hubert it distresses me to see a fellow Justice of the Peace before the court, and for driving at the excessive speed of twenty miles an hour, which, if I may say so, is more than a little precipitous. I fine you five pounds."* Then, with a twinkle in his eye worthy of Miss Marple, he looks over his spectacles: *"I suggest you stick to 'tempo giusto' in future..."* But of course he didn't and his diaries record several driving incidents! Friends of the A40 might like to know that he once drove from Gloucester to London in about three hours, and that is in the days when 'veteran' cars were new.

Maybe this is why he bought himself a bicycle, at least to use around Rustington, Littlehampton, Arundel and Angmering.

Parry was, in 1913, to compose music about the family into which his daughter Dolly had married. In *Shulbrede Times*, Dolly's husband Arthur, 1st Lord Ponsonby, was 'Father Playmate'. Saying of his son-in-law in 1917, he was 'all sorts of delightful things – a great companion to the children as well as a great politician and deeply interested in art and music as well'.

Parry's most well-known work, *Jerusalem*, was championed by the suffrage movement as we saw in the previous chapter and, once it entered the public domain in 1968, the song has been widely used at different events including being sung before Rugby League's Challenge Cup Final and every year at The Last Night of the Proms. Since 2004 it has been the anthem of the England cricket team.

Parry's composition is unusual in that all voices sing in unison. The song is also sung in many schools in Australia, USA and Canada as well as Great Britain (especially public schools) and in films such as *Chariots of Fire* in 1981.

The group Emerson, Lake and Palmer brought out a version of *Jerusalem* on their *Brain Salad Surgery* album, but the BBC banned it from being played over the airwaves; this version used to be played at high volume at home by my eldest son Andrew in the 1970s.

Photo of Knightscroft House in 2015. (46)

On 29th July 1918, after the invariable scramble, Parry left town for Rusty, where, with the exception of a few hours in town on 6th August, and three days with his daughter at Shulbrede (August 13th-16th), he spent the remaining weeks of his life at Knightscroft. He took his last bicycle ride on 6th September when he cycled to Jack Upperton's Gibbet and The Decoy, Angmering, with his student Emily Daymond.

His died on the evening of 7th October. He was cremated, and his ashes were placed in the crypt of St. Paul's

Cathedral after a memorial service. The cathedral was crowded from door to door. The music was said to be absolutely sublime and while it was a great national tribute to his genius, there was something intimate and personal about it all.

From every account of Parry we read, we gather that he was the most good-humoured, friendly and cheerful man, his favourite saying being, *"The happiest people are those who have the widest outlook."*

A true gentleman, an accomplished musician, teacher and composer!

Unveiling the blue plaque for Sir Hubert Parry outside Knightscroft House in Sea Lane by Laura Ponsonby (great granddaughter of Sir Hubert Parry and Lady Maude) (left), pictured with Bev and Mary Taylor. (47)

JM BARRIE

The Rustington connection with JM Barrie appears to have begun with the fact that Sir Hubert Parry and Maude were old friends of the Llewelyn Davies family. Maude had a great liking and admiration for Margaret, Arthur's mother.

Dolly Parry wrote a lot about the Llewelyn Davies and du Maurier families in her diaries from her teenage years onwards. Dolly first described Arthur Llewelyn Davies in 1889, the year he and Sylvia first met saying, *"Arthur Davies arrived – he is very handsome and nice, with a great deal of sense of humour..."* Dolly also described the du Mauriers as a fun-loving lot. The Parrys and du Mauriers would often attend garden parties in the village, sometimes at the Urlin's house, The Grange. Dolly mentions Guy du Maurier, who was a year older than his sister Sylvia, as being one of the cleverest and most delightful of human beings; he would sing 'delicious comic songs in a soft, low voice, and accompaniments, in the minor keys, made up by himself'. Guy was to go on to be a playwright before becoming an army officer in the Great War. He was killed in action in Flanders in 1915. The other brother she mentions is Gerald who was just three years older than Dolly. She refers to Gerald as a dear, dear thing and that he is 'so sweet to have in the house. Always happy, singing at the piano, or sitting in the garden...' He was to go on to become an actor/manager and was the father of Daphne du Maurier.

After Arthur Llewelyn Davies and Sylvia du Maurier became engaged in 1890, they went to stay with the Parrys in October 1891 in Knightscroft House. Dolly's entries in her diary from the 10th-12th October 1891, describes their developing relationship:

Saturday 10th: Arthur and Sylvia arrive.

Sunday 11th: Arthur spent this morning cutting down trees. We have never seen such a pair of undemonstrative lovers as Sylvia and Arthur. They hardly ever speak to each other even when in a room by themselves. Sylvia is a delightful thing... She is always dancing about the room. And she and I are always imitating Julia and Fred Terry. [Authors' note: Julia Neilson and Fred Terry were famous actors at that time.]

Monday 12th: Arthur cut down trees again... Sylvia and I sat down on the beach in the morning. Spent the afternoon in the music room with Sylvia and humbugged to any extent. Sylvia being Fred Terry and I Julia. Took Sylvia to see the Macfarlanes. We were ushered into the awful drawing room, and Sylvia nearly burst with laughing at the extraordinary furniture. The Humbug said to Flora 'What a pretty house,' and then made a face at me. She is great friends with Father, and says he is a 'sweet man'. Arthur says he can't bear women to like men better than their own sex, it always means there is something horrid in their characters. Love was always blind!

How ironic then was it that Arthur and Sylvia were to go on to live at Cudlow House, the house that the Macfarlanes owned!

Dolly was fascinated by Sylvia, who was ten years her senior. She found her to be amusing, mocking and captivating, whereas in her relationship with Arthur she was quiet, secretive and somewhat dreamy.

It appears from reading further entries in her diaries that other people were starting to have doubts about their compatibility, her own sister Gwen even saying that he was too dull and commonplace for Sylvia.

Nevertheless, Arthur and Sylvia were married in August 1892 and their first son George was born the following July. When Sylvia was eight months pregnant with her second child, John, they returned to Rustington, this time renting Mill House at the sea end of Sea Lane.

Barrie's connection with the family appears to date back to when he would meet the Llewellyn-Davies boys in Kensington Gardens. Sometime later Barrie was at a dinner party where he was seated next to Sylvia and their friendship began when he realised who she was.

Barrie married in the town of his birth, Kirriemuir, Scotland, in 1894, and he and his actress wife Mary first came to Rustington in 1899, renting The Firs, following Agnes Garrett's departure, half a mile from Mill House.

In 1900, Mary Barrie found Black Lake Cottage in Farnham, Surrey, which she eventually purchased for use as a holiday home. The Llewelyn Davieses then rented a 'charming cottage' in Tilford just a five-minute walk away from Black Lake Cottage. It was in this area that Tinker Bell was 'born'.

Sylvia's mother, Emma du Maurier, rented Cudlow House following the departure of the Parrys to their new house Knightscroft, nearly opposite. At this time Arthur, Sylvia and the boys regularly stayed here during the summer months and Barrie was a frequent visitor.

The rear of Cudlow House. (48)

Although Arthur did not encourage the ongoing friendship of Sylvia and their sons with Barrie, and at this time did not share their fondness for him, he did little to stand in the way of Barrie's frequent visits to their home.

JM Barrie would often play games, including cricket, with the Llewellyn Davies boys (George, John (known as Jack), Peter, Michael and Nicholas (known as Nico)) in the garden at Cudlow House. To the boys he was known as 'Uncle Jim'. The Llewelyn Davies family were to become the inspiration for the Darling family in Peter Pan.

It was here in 1906 at Cudlow House that Barrie began to think of having a statue of Peter Pan commissioned. Barrie himself took a series of photographs of Michael Llewelyn Davies (his favourite son of Arthur and Sylvia) to give to the prospective sculptor George Frampton as an idea of what Peter Pan should look like. All the pictures were taken in the garden of Cudlow House. The final work is situated in Kensington Gardens but Barrie was never happy with the finished article as Frampton used another boy as the model. Barrie had an Old English Sheepdog called Porthos, who was the inspiration for Nana in *Peter Pan.*

Left, looking down the driveway to the front of Cudlow House from a sale brochure in 1932. (49)

Right: The Peter Pan Statue in Kensington Gardens. (50)

Left: Blue plaque for James Matthew Barrie outside where Cudlow House once stood. (51)

The postcard shows Cudlow House, where JM Barrie stayed with the Llewelyn Davies family. The reverse side of the postcard below has been written and signed by JM Barrie. The card also mentions his friends Lady Maud Parry and Dolly Ponsonby (daughter of Sir Hubert Parry and Lady Maud). (52 & 53)

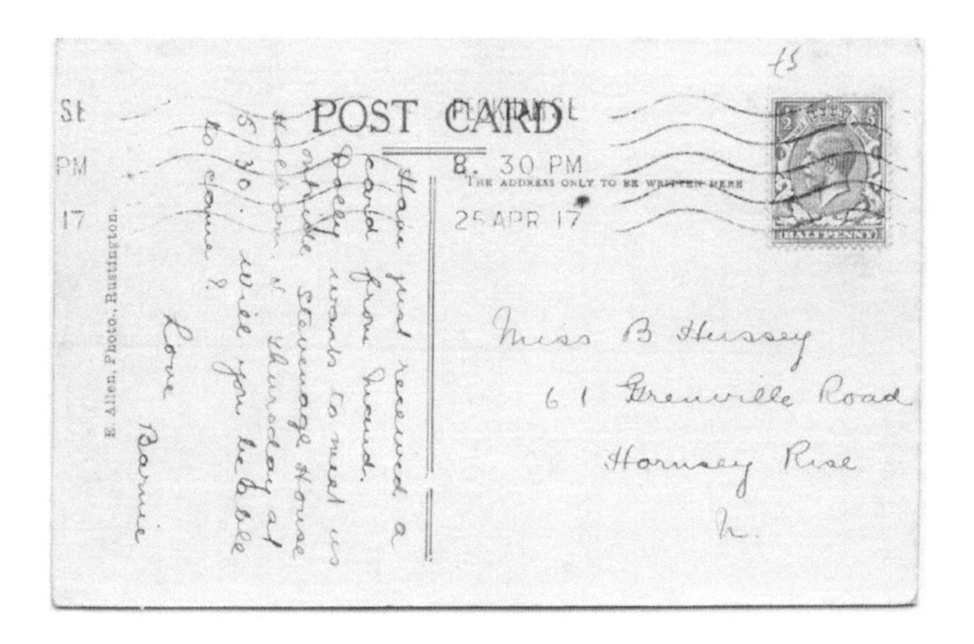

In 1906, Arthur Llewelyn Davies discovered a growth on his cheek which turned out to be a malignant sarcoma; this resulted in him having two operations. During the operations, Arthur had much of his upper jaw removed along with palate, cheek bone and tear duct on the offending side. This left him disfigured, unable to talk and in considerable pain despite having an artificial jaw insert.

JM Barrie at this time had become wealthy from his books and plays and he paid for Arthur's medical care and became a regular bedside companion, especially in the final few months of his life when Arthur lost his battle with cancer on 19th April 1907.

Sylvia welcomed Barrie's financial and emotional support for her and the boys. Just three years later Sylvia became ill with an inoperable chest cancer and died on 27th August 1910. Shortly before her death she named Barrie as one of the children's legal guardians along with her mother Emma, her brother Guy and Arthur's brother Crompton, whilst leaving the boy's nurse, Mary Hodgson, to continue caring for them. Barrie continued to give financial support to the family.

Photo taken by JM Barrie of Michael Llewelyn Davies dressed as Peter Pan in the garden at Cudlow House in 1906. (54)

Tragedy was to later strike the family; George was killed in action in Flanders aged just 21 on 15th March 1915. On 19th May 1921, less than a month before his 21st birthday, Michael, who was a student at Christ Church, Oxford, drowned along with a friend in Sandford Lasher, just downstream from Sandford Lock on the River Thames near Oxford.

On 17th September 1959, John (Known as Jack) died aged 65; he had served in the Royal Navy in the North Atlantic during the Great War. He died several months before Peter committed suicide on 5th April 1960. Barrie had publicly identified him as being the source of the name of the title character of *Peter Pan*; this identification plagued him for the rest of his life. At the time of his death he had been compiling what he called *The Morgue*, a collection of letters and family papers. In 1926, he had founded the publishing house Peter Davies Ltd.

Nicholas (Nico) joined his brother Peter's publishing company in 1935; he died aged 76 on 14th October 1980.

JM Barrie (as Hook) and Michael Llewelyn Davies (as Peter Pan) at Cudlow House, 1906. (55)

Right: JM Barrie and Sylvia Llewelyn Davies playing tennis at Cudlow, 1905. (56)

Left: Cricket on the Cudlow lawn with Michael, Smee and Nico, 1906. (57)

Corner of Sea Road and Sea Lane showing Mill House to the right of the windmill. (58)

Right and below left: Sylvia at Mill House in Sea Lane, Rustington, 1898. (59 & 60)

Right: To the left of the mill are the buildings owned by the Metropolitan Asylums Board, including Millfield House. This is now the site of the Millfield Overstrand Estate. (61)

Above: Sylvia and Michael on Rustington Beach, 1906. (62)

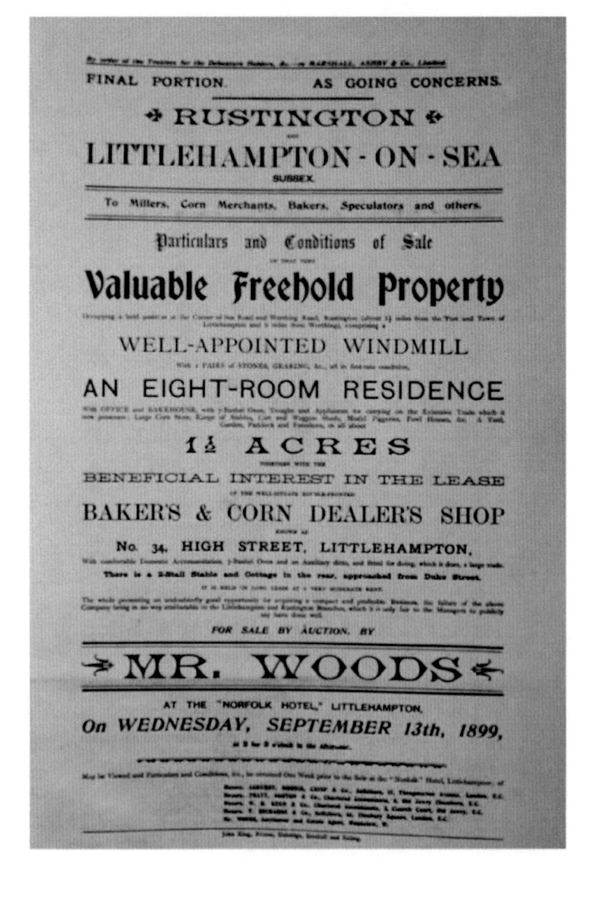

FINAL PORTION. AS GOING CONCERNS.

RUSTINGTON

LITTLEHAMPTON - ON - SEA

SUSSEX.

To Millers, Corn Merchants, Bakers, Speculators and others.

Particulars and Conditions of Sale

Valuable Freehold Property

WELL-APPOINTED WINDMILL

AN EIGHT-ROOM RESIDENCE

1½ ACRES

BENEFICIAL INTEREST IN THE LEASE

BAKER'S & CORN DEALER'S SHOP

No. 34, HIGH STREET, LITTLEHAMPTON,

There is a 2-Stall Stable and Cottage in the rear, approached from Duke Street.

FOR SALE BY AUCTION, BY

MR. WOODS

AT THE "NORFOLK HOTEL," LITTLEHAMPTON,

On WEDNESDAY, SEPTEMBER 13th, 1899,

Right: Sale brochure for the windmill and the eight-room Mill House in 1899. (63)

As for Cudlow House, nothing remains of the lawns as seen in the postcard, and the original house has been converted into three cottages. There is a blue plaque saying James Matthew Barrie stayed there.

Barrie had a great love for cricket and formed the first ever celebrity team to play cricket, in 1887. Unfortunately, his writing talents far outweighed his cricketing ability. When asked to describe his bowling action once, Barrie (a slow left-armer) replied that after delivering the ball he would go and sit on the turf at mid-off and wait for it to reach the other end which 'it sometimes did'. Here below are photographs of Barrie bowling and one of him taking the wicket of Field-Marshall Douglas Haig. (64 & 65)

The team was given the unusual name of 'Allahakbarries' on the train to their first match at Shere, when Barrie realised the full extent of his players' ignorance of cricket. So he asked the two African explorers in his team, Paul du Chaillu (of *Gorilla* fame) and Joseph Thompson (who has

Thompson's Gazelle named after him), what the African for 'Heaven help us' was; they gave him 'Allah Akbar', which actually means 'God is Great'.

Authors v Artists, 22 May 1903.
Back row, L to R: E.W. Hornung, E.V. Lucas, P.G. Wodehouse, J.C. Smith, G. Charne, Sir A. Conan Doyle, Hesketh Prichard, L.D. Luard, C.M.Q. Orchardson, L.C. Nightingale, A. Kinross. *Front row*, L to R: C. Gascoyne, Shan F. Bullock, G. Hillyard Swinstead, Reginald Blomfield, Hon. W.J. James, E.A. Abbey, A. Chevalier Taylor, J.M. Barrie, G.C. Ives, G. Spencer Watson, (sitting on ground) A.E.W. Mason.

Team photo in 1903. (66)

His team was to later include such players as Jerome K Jerome, author of *Three Men in a Boat*; P G Wodehouse, the man behind *Jeeves and Wooster*; *Winnie the Pooh* author AA Milne; and Sir Arthur Conan Doyle, the creator of *Sherlock Holmes*. Conan Doyle was a fine cricketer and played for the MCC on a number of occasions. (Gibson & Chalke, 2013)

However, the team were brought to an end by the outbreak of The Great War. A few of the younger players in the team were killed during the war, including, in 1915, the 21-year-old George Llewelyn Davies. He appeared in the team photograph for their final match in 1913.

Barrie wrote a book on his celebrity team called *Allahakbarries CC* in 1890; it was revised in 1899 and reprinted in 1950 with a forward by his personal friend Sir Donald Bradman, the legendary Australian batsman, and in

1930, following Barrie's 70th birthday, two of the great Australian players at the time, Arthur Mailey (the leg spinner) and Charlie Macartney (the hard-hitting batsman) played for a team calling itself 'Allahakbarries' for the day in his home town of Kirriemuir. Macartney was to go on to score 101 not out that day. (Barrie, 1950)

Barrie was to be awarded freedom of the town of Kirriemuir.

JM Barrie died on 19th June 1937 and was buried alongside his family on the hill in Kirriemuir, not far away from the cricket pitch where he had learnt to play and where he had given the town and cricket club a new pavilion in 1930.

Whilst doing our research, we realised that Graeme is pictured and named in the same book as JM Barrie. The book in question is *Gentleman, Gypsies and Jester... The Wonderful World of Wandering Cricket* by Anthony Gibson and Stephen Chalke. (Graeme plays for Harry Baldwin Occasionals – a team made famous by the book *Fatter Batter*, written by the actor and author Michael Simkins. (Simkins, 2008))

Above: Rod Suddaby bowling for the Baldwins at Arundel Castle. (67)

Baldwins' team picture tribute to our great friend Rod Suddaby, former Keeper of the Department of Documents at the Imperial War Museum, who initially helped encourage Graeme towards obtaining information to help write this book. (68)

Rod Suddaby (1946-2013). (69)

THE WELLESLEYS AND THE BURNABYS

As we have previously mentioned there are at least two other families who were related to royalty. The Wellesley family lived for many months of the year at Ffynches Lodge.

Ffynches Lodge. (70)

The family living there comprised of Gerald Edward Wellesley (1846-1915), his wife Ada Hamilton Martin (1852-1933) who was the 3rd daughter of James Martin, of The Upper Hall, Ledbury, Herefordshire, and their children, Viscountess Georgiana Victoria Wellesley (1881-1930) and Gerald Valerian Wellesley (1885-1961).

Gerald Edward Wellesley was the great-grandson of Garrett Wellesley (Viscount Wellesley of Dangen, and Earl of Mornington) and his wife Anne Hill Trevor. This nobleman died on 22nd May 1781, leaving seven sons. The eldest, Richard, was the 2nd Earl of Mornington, and was the 2nd great-grandfather of Queen Elizabeth, The Queen Mother. The fifth son was Arthur Wellesley, born 1st May 1769, better known as The Duke of Wellington. Henry Wellesley (1st Baron Cowley), grandfather of Gerald, was the youngest son of Garrett and Anne; he was born at the family home at Dangen Castle in the County of Meath, Ireland, in 1773.

Gerald's parents were the Rt. Hon. William Henry George Wellesley and Amelia St. John Niblock. He is buried in the Rustington Parish Church graveyard; his gravestone shows the family crest. (71)

In 1926, JM Barrie had a limited edition presentation copy of the book *The Physiology of Taste*, by Brillat-Savarin, and gave the book to Mrs Ada Hamilton Wellesley. He signed the book with the following inscription: *"Mrs Wellesley, with affectionate greetings from J. M. Barrie."*

Gerald and Ada's daughter, Georgiana, married The Right Honourable Viscount de Vescy, Ivo Richard de Vesey.

Their son, Gerald Valerian, married Elizabeth Thornton Ball and died at Highfield Park, Withyham in East Sussex.

The second family with a royal connection were living at Walnut Tree House.

Colonel Sparrow and Mrs Sparrow, who were both quite eccentric characters, lived there from the 1950s through to Mrs Sparrow's death in 1983, and her maternal cousin Anne Burnaby lived in the flat to the rear of the house.

Colonel Walter John Sparrow (1910-1979) owned a number of Aston Martin sports cars. However, it is his wife and her cousin Anne who were both 4th cousins to Queen Elizabeth, The Queen Mother. Mrs Sparrow was born Gladys Miriam Joan Larking in March 1899 at Brampton Manor in Hertfordshire; she was the daughter of Lambert Cecil Larking and Adelaide Emily Louise Burnaby.

One of the many Aston Martins Colonel Sparrow owned. (72)

Mrs Sparrow first married Rupert Darnley Swithun Anderson in 1921, son of Rupert Darnley Anderson OBE, who played football for Old Etonians and once for England; he unfortunately missed his team's FA Cup final triumph in 1879 through injury. Mrs Sparrow filed for divorce in 1929.

She remarried in 1939 to Cecil HWB Kerr and went on to marry Colonel Sparrow in 1951.

Both Mrs Sparrow and Anne Burnaby had the same grandparents, namely Reverend Henry Fowke Burnaby and his wife Louisa Jane Davy.

Both were also cousins to Frederick Gustavus Burnaby who was a traveller, writer and soldier. There is a memorial obelisk to him at St. Philip's Cathedral in Birmingham.

Anne's father was George Davy Burnaby, an actor known as 'Davy Burnaby'. His first appearance on the stage was at the Imperial Theatre on December 8th 1902 at a command performance given by Mrs Lillie Langtry before King Edward

VII; he then accompanied her to the United States in 1903. He acted in over thirty films; he starred with Stanley Holloway in the 1929 British concert musical film *The Co-optimists*, which he devised in 1921 as a stage musical where troupes of actors and singers would tour the seaside resorts of England. (Hennessey, 2005)

Davy Burnaby died (on the same day as fellow actor Will Hay who he had previously acted with) in his sleep at Walnut Tree House on 18th April 1949 following a visit from his home in Cheltenham.

Davy's daughter, Miss Jane Burnaby, was married in Rustington Church in December 1942 to Captain David B Wallace of the Royal Canadian Pay Corps.

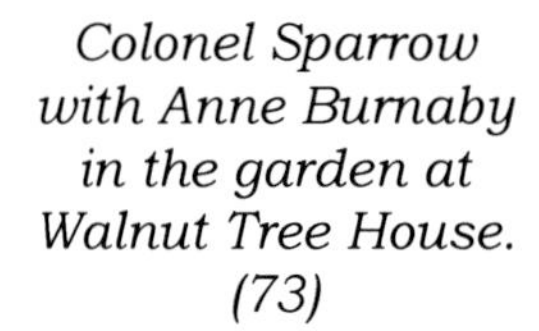

Colonel Sparrow with Anne Burnaby in the garden at Walnut Tree House. (73)

Anne Burnaby was a successful script writer, mostly in the 1950s and 1960s. However, at this time she was drinking heavily and taking drugs and, following an affair with her cousin's husband Colonel Sparrow, she stabbed him (not fatally) on Littlehampton High Street on 4th April 1960. She was sentenced for a year which she served in Holloway Prison and then at Askham Grange Open Prison in Yorkshire. In an interview with the press at the time she said Holloway had saved her life, as she was in such a mess. Following her release she went on to script write the Diana Dors film about prison life called *The Weak and the Wicked*.

SCRIPT-WRITER ANNE (SHE STABBED COLONEL) GOES BACK TO WORK

Express Staff Reporter

THE woman who wrote the script for the Diana Dors film about prison life—"The Weak and the Wicked" said yesterday: "Jail has saved my life."

Anne Burnaby, 38-year-old daughter of the late Davy Burnaby of "Co-Optimists" fame, said: "I was a mess. I took drugs. I drank too much. I would have finished with my head in the gas oven or with a murder on my hands by now if it had not been for Holloway."

A year ago she was sentenced for stabbing 49-year-old Colonel Walter John Sparrow in the back while he walked down a street in Littlehampton.

For 11 months Anne lived in, Holloway Prison and Askham Grange Open Prison in Yorkshire.

Now she is free — and going back to work on the film script of a Nigel Balchin novel for the Boulting Brothers.

She chain-smoked yesterday as she peeled potatoes for dinner at her sister's home in Mill Hill, Middlesex.

The danger

"Thank heavens that today I can say I am in control of myself again," she said. "After working on that Diana Dors film I had the most awful visions of prison life.

"But to my surprise I had a thoroughly good time. The prison officers were jolly good girls, some of whom have become my friends.

"The real danger of prisons—and I have seen it again and again — is, I believe, that too many people want to go back."

She spent her time in Holloway between the kitchens and painting Noddy dolls for the toy shops.

Anne and her husband, film publicity man John Southwood, have two sons.

She is now working on a TV play of prison life.

And Colonel Sparrow? "I have not seen him or heard from him—and that is how I propose to let the matter rest," she said.

Anne Burnaby. After prison—a film script

COLONEL SPARROW
Stabbed in the street

Cutting from the Daily Express. (74)

In Mrs Sparrow's latter years, when she was a little hard of hearing, Graeme would walk her dogs, Penny, Tessa and Two-Pence. When Graeme was first introduced to her by his brother Andrew, who used to do some gardening round there for her, she asked his name. He said, *"Graeme"*, and she replied, *"Gingerbread, that's an unusual name, what's your surname?" "Taylor"*, *"Gingerbread Trailer!"* It has been a family joke ever since. My granddaughter Bethany even made him a gingerbread trailer cake last Christmas!

Walnut Tree House in 1976. (75)

THE GENTLEMAN VICAR AND THE CONTROVERSIAL VICAR

It has been said of the Reverend Edmund Stansfield, that he was a real gentleman in every sense of the word. In 1840, when just 17 years of age, he entered Sandhurst to be gazetted an ensign in the 51st Regiment of Foot, later to serve as a lieutenant until leaving the army in 1846. After taking his BA at Downing College, Cambridge, he became curate at Mells, Somerset and whilst in this parish he founded the church at Vobster (from where the Formula One racing driver Jenson Button originates) and personally carved the pew ends.

After this he became the vicar of Donnington, Chichester, where he painted the Crucifixion over the chancel arch and Bishop Durnford later presented to him the living of Rustington. He was a greatly loved vicar here in the village between the years 1871 and 1907.

Reverend Edmund Stansfield. (76)

A well-respected gentleman with a large and happy family, he loved carving wood and produced much of the carving to be seen inside the church; these include the golden dove above the font, a bird carved in the front of the pulpit and a beautifully carved figure above the Aumbry (a small secure chest/cupboard) in the north wall of the Sanctuary.

Carving by the Reverend Stansfield above the Aumbrey. (77)

One wonders if the Reverend Edmund Stansfield would be turning in his grave if he knew that the present incumbent has decided to have the church re-ordered. This would include the removal of the pews, pulpit and other ancient artefacts in order to install new under-floor heating. The Reverend Stansfield also composed music, including 20 published hymn tunes in 1898, intended for alternative use to the tunes of *Ancient and Modern Hymns.* (We have a copy of this booklet in our collection.)

Carvings by Rev. Stansfield.

Left: At the front of the pulpit. (78)

Below Dove above the font. (79)

(80)

However, he was most noted for his kindness and generosity; a real father figure to all his parishioners. If he was told that one of his male parishioners had been injured or taken ill, he would immediately set off and visit them, taking a bottle of wine for them; if it was a lady who was ill or had recently had a baby, he would visit them, taking flowers and a large basket of fruit and groceries. The Reverend Stansfield always paid for these out of his own pocket. We understand that he was quite a wealthy gentleman.

The Reverend Stansfield was very sadly missed by the people of the village when he died; his plain flat gravestone can still be seen quite near the north door of the church, with just the letters E.S. on it. There is also a stained glass window of St. Edmund in the Lady Chapel dedicated to him (see opposite). (81)

The flats on the corner of Mill Lane with Station Road are named after him and known today as Stansfield Court.

Note The Vicarage at this time was the very large flint built house on the south side of The Street, now Numbers 83 and 85, The Street. Number 85 is today the Abbots Wood Dental Surgery, while No. 83 is a private residence. To the west of these two properties is the old flint Coach House (No. 81); this property has now been converted into a private residence, but has kept its name.

The next vicar to come to Rustington Church, in 1908, was the Reverend James Louis Crosland. His appointment was to prove controversial and the subsequent events during his time at the parish are finally being documented.

Reverend James Louis Crosland. (82)

However, we would like to give you a synopsis of this gentleman's early life, including the political flavour at the time, which as you'll discover towards the end, was of a very different nature to that at the beginning of this story.

James Louis Crosland was born on 23rd September 1867 in Lockwood, Crosland Moor in Huddersfield. (Crosland Moor is a district named after the family who were landowners here in the 15th and 16th centuries.) James grew up with seven siblings, two brothers and five sisters. As with nearly all the families living here at the time, most of them, when they were old enough, were employed at one of the local woollen mills. The Crosland family was no exception. Their father, Walter John Crosland, was a woollen cloth dresser, and nearly all of his eight children were either at school or working down at the mill as mill hands, that is apart from the elder brother Charles, who became a joiner/cabinet maker.

In 1891, with James Louis Crosland now aged 24, he broke away from the family and the mill, and we find him training to become a Church of England clergyman at St. Bee's Theological College in Cumberland.

A year later, just after his 25th birthday, James was being ordained a Deacon, by the Bishop of Wakefield. He was then appointed as Curate of All Souls Church, in Halifax. This appointment would have seen James being elevated into the ranks of the middle class and would have enabled him to become involved in local politics and musical events. In 1894, on his 27th birthday, James was ordained a Priest at Wakefield Cathedral, by Dr Walsham How, the Bishop of Wakefield. Later, Crosland was appointed to St. Augustine's in Halifax where he remained until 1905.

Meanwhile, the political landscape was very interesting at this time, not only women's suffrage as we have already discussed and the Anglo-Boer wars but also Home Rule for Ireland came to dominate British politics from 1885 to the start of the Great War. In 1880, William Gladstone became

Prime Minister as the Liberal Party took power from Benjamin Disraeli's Conservatives and held office until 1885. The Conservatives won the next election, forming a minority government under Robert Gascoyne-Cecil, 3rd Marquis of Salisbury. Gladstone re-took power in 1886 and during this year he introduced the First Home Rule Bill for Ireland; however, he was defeated in Parliament not just by the Conservatives but also the Liberal Party who split between pro- and anti-Home Rule MPs. Following this vote, the Liberals lost the resulting General Election and it kept them out of power for the next six years. When they came back to power in 1892, the Home Bill Rule was reintroduced in 1893; this time it passed the House of Commons but was rejected by the House of Lords, which resulted in Gladstone's resignation.

Mr. William Rawson-Shaw, M.A., J.P.

(83)

The sitting MP for Halifax, since the 1882 by-election, was Thomas Shaw, a Liberal politician, married to Elizabeth Rawson; they lived at the Allangate Mansion in Halifax. He went on to hold this seat until his death in 1893, aged 69. His father owned the Brookroyd Mills. A year before his election success, on the coming of age of his son William Rawson Shaw, Thomas Shaw gave £1,000 to the Halifax School Board to promote education in Halifax. This money was used to set up the Rawson Shaw Scholarships. (http://www.digplanet.com/wiki/Thomas Shaw (MP), 2014)

William Rawson Shaw was a highly intelligent man who had previously worked as a political private secretary and had married the daughter of an MP following the death of his father. He fought and won the resulting by-election on behalf of the Liberal Party (*Portsmouth Evening News*, 1893). He was also a magistrate in Yorkshire and a proponent of progressive education in schools. Despite the Liberal Party losing the 1895 election, William held on to his seat. However, Rawson Shaw found that working as a magistrate was preferable to the cut and thrust of politics and as a result resigned his seat in 1897 and moved south to live in Rustington, where he became Chairman of the Arundel Bench of Magistrates, a position he held for the next 14 years. He called his house Allangate after the family home in Halifax and, besides his duties on the bench, he would support many local charities, clubs and institutions.

During the 1890s, the Liberal Party in the West Riding of Yorkshire had been working hand in glove with the Church of England in an attempt to gain votes from the Conservatives and the newly emerging Labour Party. Whereas the Church was trying to increase the size of its congregations, in competition with the various non-conformist churches and the worrying rise of indifference to any religious belief at all. Both the Liberal Party and the Church could claim to be building Jerusalem, among the dark satanic mills, the former by way of social reforms and the latter through moralistic guidance and charitable work.

(Some of the words were taken from William Blake's preface to his epic *Milton a Poem*, better known as *Jerusalem*, written just eight miles away from Rustington, in Felpham.) Music would have been one avenue used by both the politicians and the clergy to help achieve their respective goals.

William Rawson-Shaw's home Allangate. (84)

James Crosland spent some of his ministerial time at All Souls Church, Halifax, organising concerts of both religious and secular music in the church hall, where he would have been in contact with the Shaws. It was here that he met his first wife Letitia Moore, who had an exquisite soprano voice. Letitia was the daughter of Henry Edwin Moore, an organist and Professor of Music and her mother Sarah Ann Shaw was also a vocalist. Letitia was at the time a star vocalist of the musical performers based at Leeds Parish Church which toured the various parishes of the West Riding. She became a professional singer and sung several times in concerts at the Albert Hall (*Leeds Mercury*, 1885). They were married in 1901 at a Civil Registry Office. We have not been able to ascertain the reason for this, but it is likely that either the Moore family did not approve of the match or that Letitia wanted to keep her private life hidden from her public image as a professional singer. Sadly it appears that Letitia died just five years later aged 38 in September 1904, at Lytham in Lancashire.

After the sadness of losing his wife, instead of requesting a transfer from the Diocese of Wakefield to another parish on compassionate grounds, James decided to leave the area, and follow William Rawson Shaw down to Sussex to make a fresh start. By the time James arrived, Rawson Shaw would have been well established in the village. James was appointed Curate in Charge of St. Mary's Church in East Preston and also to an attached chapel in Ferring. Whilst there, East Preston assumed the status of an independent parish of which James became the first vicar. It was now 1905 and he was living at Roundstone House in East Preston, a house just to the north-east of the railway level crossing in Old Worthing Road, East Preston.

Roundstone House – Home of James Louis Crosland prior to him becoming the Vicar of Rustington. (85 & 86)

Between 1905 and 1908, there are reports in the local press of well-organised parish fetes at Roundstone House, with singing and musical accompaniment a noticeable feature, showing that James's talents for organising such events had not been left in Halifax.

Following the death of the Reverend Edmund Stansfield, Crosland's name had been put forward as the new vicar. However, the two churchwardens had their own candidate for the new vicar in mind. A strenuous campaign to oppose the appointment of James Crosland was mounted by the churchwardens, especially by the senior churchwarden, Edward Gerald Penfold Wyatt, which eventually resulted in the Lord Chancellor having to make the final decision.

Rustington Hall, the home of Edward Gerald Penfold Wyatt. (87)

Wyatt was a very prominent person in Rustington, a Justice of the Peace and a governor of the local school which had been endowed by one of his ancestors. He was to later write the following books: *St Gregory and the Gregorian Music* in 1904; *English or Roman Use?* in 1913; and co-author with the Anglican priest, Arthur Duncan-Jones and Stephen

Gaselee, a diplomat, the book *A Directory of Ceremonial* in 1921. Wyatt had moved to the village in 1900 and had set about modernising Rustington Hall and its staff accommodation. When he took up residence he would have been virtually neighbours with Rawson Shaw at Allangate.

The reasons for their objections to the curate becoming vicar included a mixture of both political and personal prejudice. He was moving down from a Liberal stronghold area to a strongly pro-Conservative one; his humble beginnings; his training at St. Bees; his association with his rival Rawson Shaw (Wyatt was worried that they would try to reform the Rustington School, a church school under the vicar's rule, and remove his family's connection with it); and his short marriage to a professional singer to name but a few.

The living was given by the Lord Chancellor during the vacancy in the See, to James Louis Crosland, the Yorkshire man. So, in March 1908, the Reverend James Louis Crosland was promoted to Vicar of Rustington.

In the Rustington School logbook there is an entry on 2nd March 1908, written by the schoolmistress, stating that the new vicar called to introduce himself. As part of his role as vicar he was now in charge of the school. Rustington School brought together both Crosland and Rawson Shaw, the vicar teaching religious instruction and testing the pupils on their knowledge of the Bible, whilst Mr and Mrs Rawson Shaw took a more paternalistic approach to the pupils' progress; he assessing the children's general knowledge, especially in history and geography, and she judging the girls' achievements in sewing and other handicrafts. Wyatt's fears were coming to fruition.

Although the new vicar appeared to be well received at Rustington School, the same cannot be said of the church. He was not readily accepted by the officials of the vestry, the churchwardens. One would expect their loyalty to the previous incumbent, especially if they thought Crosland would be trying to change working practices, but over time, Crosland's personality and man-management skills should have been sufficient to overcome these initial difficulties. However, the problems in the vestry were not easing.

Representations were made by the churchwardens to the Bishop of Chichester to have James Crosland removed. The bishop would have been aware of their objections when Crosland's name had been originally proposed but was not in a position to overrule the Lord Chancellor's judgement.

However, by 1909, fresh allegations were being made against the Reverend Crosland that he had misappropriated funds from the Parish Poor Relief Fund for his own use. This forced the vicar to take rather hasty action to clear his name by gaining support from many of the Poor in Relief of the village. The churchwardens reported the vicar's action to the Bishop (of Chichester), who backed away from the infighting in the parish, saying that it was a matter for the civil court.

Mr EGP Wyatt launched his prosecution of the vicar by fraud. The Magistrates' Court proceedings were reported blow by blow in the *Chichester Observer* newspaper between 26th January and 16th February 1910. The case was also reported in many other newspapers, some printing the more amusing comments made by the villagers of Rustington under oath.

SERIOUS CHARGE AGAINST THE VICAR OF RUSTINGTON

Reads the Headline

ALLEGED FRAUD

There was much local interest displayed on Thursday at the Arundel Town Hall, in the hearing of the charge against the Vicar of Rustington (The Rev. James Louis Crosland). A great many rumours had been rife in the village for some months, and this had culminated in the vicar being summoned, with the charge that he, between April 20th 1908 and April 12th

1909, did fraudulently use for his own purposes, cash collected for the benefit of the sick and poor of the village.

One of the Churchwardens, (he had been so for 8 years) of the Church, Mr E.G.P Wyatt, (Chairman of Rustington Parish Council), who lived at Rustington Hall, brought the charge against the vicar.

It seems from questions put to members of the public who should be in receipt of the funds donated, that the vicar did come and gave out some cash to them, but that the vicar did cover the amount shown in the book with his thumb, and that he asked them to sign their name to say that had received certain monies. Whether this was what was recorded in the book, they did not know. There were many columns of statements from the public.

Later in February, the case against the Vicar was dismissed, so this was presumably the end of the matter. Following the decision, Mr E.G.P. Wyatt then resigned as Churchwarden.

When the fraud case failed to remove Crosland, he temporarily vacated the parish and moved up to Kensington as there had been a certain amount of fallout in the newspapers. Following the fraud case, Crosland had become a minor celebrity up in London and was in hot demand in London society circles. The widower had another thing on his mind, a certain lady that he was courting; she was to become his wife just a few months later at Holy Trinity Church, Kensington Gore. The lady in question was Constance Humphrey Davidson who was 32 (a good ten years younger than him) and they were married on 27th September 1910. Like his first wife, James Crosland had found himself another vocalist and musician.

Constance was from a rich and well-connected family, whose fortune had been generated from trading in the East Indies, as her father and later her brother, George Ireland Humphrey Davidson, had been partners of Ireland, Fraser and Co., General Merchants and Commission Agents in

Mauritius. Ireland was also Constance's grandmother's maiden name. Constance was the daughter of George Walter Davidson and Johanna; she had several brothers and sisters. Politically the Davidsons were pro-Conservative, being part of the ruling establishment; they used their wealth to maintain their social position and obtain careers for their sons in the armed forces, the civil service and the law. The Davidson girls were raised to marry well; Constance and a younger sister were presented at Court in 1900, curtsying before Queen Victoria at Buckingham Palace. Although the family were Scottish, Constance was born at The Castle, in Mauritius, in the Indian Ocean. (MacMillan, 2000)

James Crosland could now be viewed as a respected member of the establishment; he had been cleared of a false charge of criminality and now had a well-connected wife with a pro-Conservative family. Therefore, Crosland had now become the ideal candidate for the role of vicar that his detractors had demanded in 1908.

Looking at the Census Returns of April 1911, the vicar and his wife were living at the Rustington Vicarage where they were to stay for the next thirty years. They kept two live-in staff, Ann Kibble (the cook) and Annie Stannard (the house parlour maid). (1911 England Census (database online), 2011)

The vicar and his wife were blessed with a baby son on October 17th 1911, born in Kensington and they chose the names John Sidney George. He was christened in the church at Rustington by his father on December 19th 1911. He was now a future heir to a part of his grandfather's fortune on his mother's side. John Sidney George Crosland spent much of his early life away from Rustington with his mother's family who had him privately educated.

Prior to the appointment in 1930 of Mr Healey as organist, Mr Crosland trained the choir himself, with the help of Constance. This seems to have been a very successful venture, as many awards came to Rustington Church Choir at the Annual Festivals of West Sussex Choirs.

Jubilee Day procession 1935, James Louis Crosland pictured far left, Mr Healey on far right. Mary's Uncle Ern was the crucifer. (88)

In 1913, the vicar decided he would like choir stalls in the chancel; these were duly made and installed. However, it seems the bishop refused to grant a faculty (a necessity for any improvement, alteration or addition inside a church), so all these beautifully-carved oak stalls had to be sold off, to pay for the costs involved in the inquiry.

In the following year, 1914, came the start of the Great War of 1914-18. At this time class barriers were coming down in society as more demands were being made on the population to support the war effort.

James and Constance now had the opportunity to indulge their organisational and musical skills for the numerous fundraising concerts and other activities. *The Littlehampton Observer* reported on one such event, on 21st October 1914, as follows:

PATRIOTIC CONCERT AT RUSTINGTON

A SUCCESSFUL EFFORT

A patriotic evening concert in aid of the Rustington War Emergency Fund took place in the Lamb Hall on Tuesday, and proved to be one of the most enjoyable entertainments of its kind ever held in the village. The first part of the programme consisting of songs by Mr. Frank Flavin, "A Call to Arms" (Jack Thompson); Mrs. Roy Fabling, "She wandered down the mountain side" (Frederick Clay); Miss Henson, "When you come home" (W. H. Squire); Mr Wynne, "The British Lion" (Henry Walker); Mrs. Crosland, "Soldiers in the Park" (Lionel Monkton); Miss E. V. Richardson, "There's a land" (Frances Allitson); Master Eric Bright, "Sing, sweet bird"; Miss Nutley, "Land of hope and glory" (Elgar); Mr. G. Gallagher, "Fall in" (Cowan). All the artistes did well and the applause in each case, very hearty.

Rustington Church during the war with the blackout curtains. (89)

During the interval Mr. E. Flavin gave skilful pianoforte renderings of the National Anthems of the allies and a duet was given by Miss Luck, and Mr. W. F. Booker.

Encores were very numerous during the second section of the programme. Perhaps this was because from the start the audience woke up to the fact that an encore might prove even more popular than the item on the programme, for Mrs. Crosland's "It's a Long Way to Tipperary" fairly 'brought the house down', when it was rendered in answer to a recall for "Your King and Country want You" (Paul A. Reubens)... (*The Littlehampton Observer*, 1914)

During the war the vicar did become closer to his parishioners, especially at times of need when any bad news had come from the front concerning families from the village.

James Crosland's in-laws' (the Davidsons) military involvement in the Great War has been well documented. Constance's youngest brother, Lieutenant Colonel Edward Humphrey Davidson CBE, MC, was appointed Director of Intelligence for the Air Ministry on the formation of the RAF, and won the Military Cross, serving with the Gordon Highlanders. (His Orders and decorations were sold by Messrs. Bonham's, Knightsbridge, in September 2011 for £2,280.) One of her older brothers was Sir John Humphrey 'Tavish' Davidson KCMG, DSO, CB. John was born on 24th July 1876; he joined the army and soon became an officer. He won the DSO with the 60th Rifles in the Second Boer War (*Dundee Courier*, 1954). He was very much involved with the First World War; he joined the 111 Corps as a staff officer and participated in the first Battles of Marne, Aisne and Ypres. Following the formation of the First Army in 1915, he became Douglas Haig's operations officer. As part of that role he was the chief organiser of the Battles of Loos, Neuve Chapelle and the Second Battle of Artois. He was then promoted to Director of Military Operations on the Western Front at General Headquarters following Douglas Haig's rise to Commander-in-Chief of the British Expeditionary Force on the Western Front. After the war he was the author of the book *Haig: Master of the Field* and he also became an MP.

After the war it had become obvious that Rustington Churchyard was full, and would have to be closed for future interments. The Parish Church was originally built on the site of the old wooden Saxon church. Now, with so many burials having taken place here over the centuries, the ground had risen around three feet above the foundations of the church and that is why you have to step down in order to enter the church itself.

A new site was sought and a few offers of land were put to the vicar, but in most cases, for some reason or other, they would not have been suitable for the purpose. Miss Urlin of The Grange, Sea Lane, offered a piece of land that she owned off Worthing Road, which was accepted and eventually used, although it was never a popular burial ground, partly because of its access down a tree and hedge lined pathway, and it did not appeal as a lasting resting place for many people for their loved ones.

In actual fact it was first used in 1926, with the burial of Emma Blunden of Nelson Villa, Church Rd, Rustington. She was buried on January 1st 1926, aged 79 years. The last burial took place here in 1952, a friend of our family, Mr Henry Dolman, of Firs Cottage, The Street, Rustington. He was buried on December 24th 1952, aged 82. There were a total of 58 burials in this cemetery. Contrary to popular belief, only two of the bodies' remains have been removed from the site, the head and footstones were also taken away. One set of headstones were taken to the churchyard, and placed against the south wall. However, there were rumours going around at the time that some bodies were being removed secretly, but if so, where to? Sadly, the Worthing Road Burial Ground was always sadly neglected, and the vicar said, *"It was enough to keep up the Churchyard, without the extra cost of maintaining the Burial Ground."*

In 1919, at a Church Meeting, it was decided to install a new organ in the Parish Church, this was to be the War Memorial for the village; so far they had raised £7.19.9d out of a total cost expected to be in the region of £700. This came as a severe shock to the people of Rustington, firstly over the lack of consultation with them, and secondly, that only a small percentage of the community of Rustington would enjoy it. Eventually, a wooden ex-army hut was installed in Church Road, which could be used, and was, by all sections of the community for a wide variety of purposes, a much more suitable memorial for the village at this time, rather than a church organ.

During the war years, James and Constance could enjoy their son, John Sidney George Crosland, growing up prior to sending him away to school. Constance and James did not conform to the normal Davidson family trend, as Constance's brothers and sisters had either wielded a certain amount of power and influence or had married spouses that did. However, she did use her influence to fight for James in his disputes with the churchwardens.

In 1935, the vicar was mainly responsible for purchasing a new John Compton electric organ; this was sited at the north-west end of the nave, while the choir sat in the last two rows of pews on the other side of the aisle.

The roaring 20s saw Britain booming for the first few years having won the war; peace had returned and with it prosperity. However, it was not to last; by the mid-twenties, for a variety of reasons, the economy had declined. Demand for British products fell, unemployment more than doubled from 1 million to 2.5 million leading to the Great Strike of 1926. This led to the foundation of the Communist Party of Great Britain (CPGB) in 1920, whose membership greatly increased, especially in the mining areas following the General Strike and The Wall Street Crash in 1929, which heralded the Great Depression worldwide.

The emergence of a young Oswald Mosley, who was taking on the whole political establishment suddenly, became a cause that appealed to the Croslands. Mosley started as a Conservative MP, became disillusioned with them and stood as an Independent. He joined the Independent Labour Party in 1926; a year later he was elected to the National Executive Committee. When the Labour Government refused to endorse his plans for national reconstruction, he resigned and founded the New Party. After a disastrous 1931 for the New Party, he visited Benito Mussolini in Italy; he then disbanded the New Party and formed the British Union of Fascists (BUF) in 1932.

In 1998, Channel 4 produced a documentary series about Oswald Mosley. The part of Mosley was played by Jonathan Cake, a former pupil of the Angmering School, and Roger May played the part of John Strachey the Labour politician who was to later go on to support the Communist Party; both are friends who play for the Baldwins cricket team.

Jonathan Cake sporting a moustache for the part of Mosley is seated front right on the wall with Roger May seated 3 places to left of him in the same row. I'm the one padded up with the bat. Photo taken outside the pavilion of Lancing College. (90)

FASCISM COMES TO RUSTINGTON

We will start this chapter of events with Mary's personal recollections of what was happening in the village at the time.

Mary and Bev Taylor's wedding day at Rustington Church on 27th October 1951.

From left to right: Edgar Sopp (Bride's father); Victor Barnes (Best Man); Beverley Taylor (Groom); Mary Taylor (nee Sopp) (Bride); Muriel Taylor (Groom's mother); Elizabeth (Queenie) Sopp (Bride's mother); Arthur Taylor (Groom's father); Binnie Barnes (Bridesmaid); and George Richard Sopp (Bride's paternal grandfather). (91)

I must now digress a little, but it does concern this story. My paternal grandfather, Mr George Richard Sopp, a master builder in the Petworth area, moved with his family to Rustington in 1922, to Hawthorn in Waverley Road, and became a sub-contractor for Mr Tom Summers. They became involved with building many properties in Sea Avenue and Broadmark Lane amongst others. When he retired, he joined the Parish Church as a sidesman, and his three youngest sons (he had 9 sons and 1 daughter) became members of the church choir, and one of them became the crucifer. I myself was christened by the Reverend Crosland on 4th May 1930.

Incidentally, Graeme was also in the church choir (under choirmaster and organist, Tim 'Uncle' Healey) for very many years, under Canon Cobb before being appointed crucifer under Reverend Evans. Uncle Healey at first permitted a few ladies in the choir, one of these ladies was Dorothy whom he married after a few years of running the choir. They had become a very popular couple in the village.

Picture taken on Armistice Day 1984, Graeme as crucifer with Reverend Evans. (92)

Each year, Uncle Healey and his wife Dorothy took the choirboys away for an annual holiday, commencing just after they were married and continuing for about the next 35 years, except for the war years when 'Uncle' was serving in the RAF. For the last two of these camps Uncle Healey asked my husband Bev and I to go along with them, as by now he was getting older and needed help with the week's camping for the 20 or so boys. These camps were held in Tilford and Slinfold; Graeme was one of the choirboys at the time. Previous camps were also held at Greatstone-on-Sea and the Isle of Wight. Uncle Healey worked as Estate Manager for the Duke of Norfolk and the Duke would loan at no charge ridge tents, marquees, cooking utensils, tables and chairs, equipment etc.

In the 1970s, the choir was at its height and they even sang at St. George's Chapel in Windsor Castle.

Anyway, back to 1930, my paternal grandfather had built a house for his family in North Lane and eventually went on to build many of the houses in this road, including one for my maternal grandparents in 1932.

George Sopp also went on to become a handyman for Vicar Crosland, where he became involved in many aspects of the church, as well as at The Vicarage. One thing he did during his work here was a detailed plan of the churchyard, drawing every grave that was there then in situ; this has become so useful to us in our work, as the gravestones have largely been removed to make way for the smaller monumental inscriptions for cremations.

We contacted the original local undertakers to obtain details of the old internments within the churchyard, and were quite shocked and surprised to find they held no records as such! This is because the sexton at the church memorised these, and were of course lost when he himself sadly passed away. They did, however, pass on to us scribbled notes and casual sites where some burials did take place, along with the names, which helped in our research.

However, grandfather became more and more disenchanted with the Crosland family when they commenced entertaining some rather strange guests at The Vicarage over several years from the early 1930s. It seems the main one of these guests was one William Joyce, the infamous

Lord Haw Haw. At this time he was already known for his affiliation to the Blackshirt fraternity, under the leadership of Sir Oswald Mosley. Mosley appointed William Joyce as the British Union of Fascists' full-time propaganda director. Joyce's second wife, Margaret Cairns White, was also believed to be staying in the village, but not at The Vicarage; the whereabouts of this are still unknown.

John Sidney George Crosland and William Joyce were often to be seen, by very many local people, playing tennis together at one of the several tennis courts in Rustington, especially at the courts in Seafield Road. (Situated, where Corbett's Tyre and Exhaust Centre and the Dragon Chinese Restaurant are now.)

The political movement, The British Union of Fascism, or BUF for short, was growing in this country and The Winds of Change were not going to pass Rustington by. It seems that for some time none of the villagers knew we had one of the Blackshirt bases here in Rustington.

It was in the early 1930s that the British Union of Fascists, or the 'Blackshirts' as they were more commonly called, were becoming a nuisance all over England. Members wore completely black uniforms; young boys wore grey uniforms with leather belts, the buckles depicting the fascist symbol. These were not just drop outs from society, thugs etc., but very many men of standing, influential and respected men of society who had become mostly disenchanted with the Conservative Party. Even some of the newspapers were supporting the BUF. Two of these were the *Daily Mirror* and the *Daily Mail.* The *Mirror* had the headline *"Give the Blackshirts a helping hand"* whereas the *Mail*'s headline was *"Hurrah for the Blackshirts"*.

On the other side, in the late twenties and early thirties, was the Communist Party (CPGB) with its 'class against class policy', dubbed 'social fascists' at the time. With Hitler's victory in Germany the CPGB changed its policy to the Popular Front. This policy argued that fascism was the main danger to the workers' movement and so it allied itself with all anti-fascist forces, including right-wing democratic parties. Support for the party was at its height in the 1930s and 1940s. They were heavily involved in the Battle of Cable Street in East London on Sunday 4th October 1936. This was a clash between the Metropolitan Police who were overseeing a march by members of the BUF and various local Jewish, Irish, socialist anarchists and the CPGB. In Worthing, Labour Party members were selling the *Daily Worker*, the newspaper of the Communist Party, on the streets of the town. They were subsequently expelled from the Labour Party.

From a document HO/283/23, held at the Public Record Office at Kew, it tells that of all the counties in southern England, during the build-up before the commencement of the Second World War, West Sussex was the most important and the strongest from a fascist point of view.

Worthing was the hotbed and was known as the Munich of the South. In the early 1930s, branches of Mosley's British Union of Fascists were already being set up along this part of the West Sussex coast. These branches being in Chichester, Bognor, Littlehampton, Worthing, Burgess Hill, Horsham, Petworth and Selsey.

In Chichester they held premises in East Street and very regular meetings outside the city's market gates, whereas in Bognor meetings were held near the Marine Gardens and in Waterloo Square. In Littlehampton, the fascist newspaper, *Blackshirt*, was hawked on the corner of Beach Road and the High Street, John Sidney Crosland being one of the sellers; their headquarters was at 29 High Street, some group meetings were also being held at the Rustington Vicarage. By early 1934, 110 copies of the *Blackshirt* newspaper were sold in one week.

The Blackshirts decided to have summer camps on the south coast, at Pagham, Selsey and West Wittering. These brought in quite an amazing amount of money for their funds (running into £1,000s). The camps were for members and their families and these camps were advertised in the *Blackshirt*, stating the holiday would be near Bognor, close to the sea. There would be dancing, bathing, games both indoors and out and a restaurant. Four meals were provided a day and accommodation would be provided in large bell tents accommodating between 2 and 6 people, mainly families; these had double fly roofs which projected outwards, forming a veranda and inside wooden floors, carpets and good beds were supplied. There were separate blocks for parties of single men and women, as well as married quarters. The camps would last for about 7 to 8 weeks.

BLACKSHIRT

BRITISH UNION NEWS

PUBLISHED MONTHLY. No. 248. MARCH, 1938 Registered at G.P.O. as a newspaper. Price 1d.

HOW LANCASHIRE HEARD MOSLEY'S CALL

GREAT BRITISH UNION COTTON CRUSADE

IN the second two weeks of February more than two hundred meetings have been held in Lancashire, some in the frost, some in the wind, and some in the rain, but most in the wind and rain, and all in the bitter cold. In such weather vast audiences were an impossibility; that there were audiences at all proves the interest aroused in the Blackshirt policy for the stricken cotton industry. No other party could have attracted crowds like those that gathered round the British Union speakers on the wind-swept market places, bleak crofts, and exposed street corners of the cotton towns.

Typical of the meetings held during [illegible] by Miss Bell, in Rochdale Town Hall Square. Icy rain slanted down on a biting wind with great force. For nearly an hour and a half the crowd, drenched through, hemmed in the rostrum, [illegible]

Carroll, and Dunkerley have done particularly good work in this centre. On Merseyside, where a team of enthusiastic speakers is operating, Neville is living up to the reputation for dependability and endurance which he established for himself during the Wavertree elections.

LEATHER LUNGS

IN the northern cotton towns Sumners' leather lungs have become well known over a dozen pitches, while Eaton and O'Malley have both given practical proof of their faith by taking more meetings than were originally allotted to them. Mrs. Booth has done good work in these North Lancashire towns; while in his own particular sphere Mercer has seen to it that the public is made aware of Mosley's promise to the cotton industry.

The Leader's meetings in Platting and [illegible]

Copy of Blackshirt *newspaper being sold on street corners by JSG Crosland and others. This edition mentions Doreen Bell, mentioned later in the chapter. (93)*

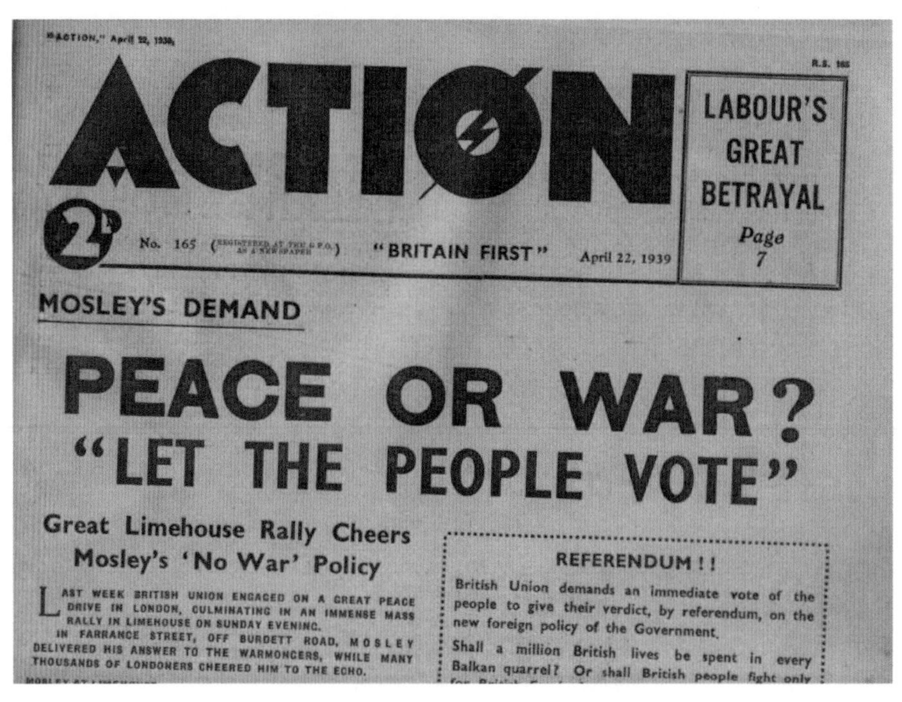

"ACTION," April 22, 1939

ACTION

2d

No. 165 "BRITAIN FIRST" April 22, 1939

LABOUR'S GREAT BETRAYAL Page 7

MOSLEY'S DEMAND

PEACE OR WAR?
"LET THE PEOPLE VOTE"

Great Limehouse Rally Cheers Mosley's 'No War' Policy

LAST WEEK BRITISH UNION ENGAGED ON A GREAT PEACE DRIVE IN LONDON, CULMINATING IN AN IMMENSE MASS RALLY IN LIMEHOUSE ON SUNDAY EVENING.

IN FARRANCE STREET, OFF BURDETT ROAD, MOSLEY DELIVERED HIS ANSWER TO THE WARMONGERS, WHILE MANY THOUSANDS OF LONDONERS CHEERED HIM TO THE ECHO.

REFERENDUM!!

British Union demands an immediate vote of the people to give their verdict, by referendum, on the new foreign policy of the Government.

Shall a million British lives be spent in every Balkan quarrel? Or shall British people fight only

The other newspaper sold by the BUF. The title of the paper was used as the motto for Bognor's coat of arms! (94)

We understand that Oswald Mosley, along with his son Nicholas, would spend at least one day at each of these popular camps. Many photographs were taken of him with various groups. He would happily enter into the life of the camp and would always go swimming. On his arrival at the camp in full uniform he would receive a welcome guard of honour and would be given the Blackshirt leader salute and a shout of 'Heil Mosley'. The fascist symbol was put up everywhere, even drawn in the sand on the beaches. The symbol was that of a large circle with a lightning flash through the centre.

The Blackshirt branch was growing strong here in Rustington well before 1934. The Women's Officer in Charge was a Mrs E King. However, the Officer in Charge overall, was a Mr John Sidney George Crosland, son of James Louis Crosland, Vicar of Rustington. He was also vicar's warden at the church and serving on Rustington Parish Council. He also represented Lyminster as a West Sussex County Councillor.

Left: John Sidney George Crosland. (95)

The Vicarage where the Croslands lived. (96)

Although the vicar described himself at this time as a non-active member of the Blackshirts, this did not prevent him from allowing many Blackshirt meetings to take place at The Vicarage.

In Littlehampton, the first meeting of many took place in 1934; one of these meetings was led by Mrs Norah Elam, the Women's County Organiser, with an audience of over 100 local women. Norah Elam (also known as Norah Dacre Fox) was a militant feminist, having been a prominent member of the Women's Social and Political Union, where she served as general secretary. She was imprisoned, in Holloway, three times between May and July 1914 for 'Acts of Terrorism' as part of the struggle as discussed in the suffrage chapter earlier.

On Tuesday 9th October 1934, both John Sidney Crosland and the vicar, James Crosland, attended Mosley's meeting at the Pavilion in Worthing. Also in attendance were William Joyce, fellow West Sussex County Councillor Captain Charles Henry Bentinck Budd and another close friend of theirs, Jorian Jenks, a farmer/author from Angmering. Jorian Jenks could very easily be said to be the father of the 'Green Party' had it not been for his involvement with the BUF. He was a proponent of sustainable and organic farming, warned of the dangers of artificial pesticides and fertilizers to the health of the public and wrote several books on the subject.

Jorian Jenks. (97)

There was widespread media coverage of the riots in the town following Mosley's meeting. Following the arrests of Sir Oswald Mosley, Joyce, Budd and Bernard Mullins (a member of the Blackshirt movement) for riotous assembly, it was reported in the *Yorkshire Evening Post* of 14th November 1938 that the Reverend James Louis Crosland was called as a witness in the case of the above defendants. It stated under the subtitle 'Vicar Supports Fascists' that *"The Rev. James Louis Crosland, Vicar of Rustington for over 28 years, said he was a 'non-active member' of the British*

Union of Fascists. He was at the meeting. Outside there was a sound of fireworks and two explosions. When he left, the crowd displayed a rather threatening attitude. He had to force his way through. There was no cordon of police, and it was a hostile crowd. Asked whether he was a supporter, witness said if it came to a choice between that and something worse he would choose the BUF. Later witness said he did not think it was Worthing people who were causing the trouble. He still thought Worthing people were respectable."

All the defendants were acquitted at the trial. (*Yorkshire Evening Post*, 1934)

It has now been revealed that the vicar himself, along with his wife, were in fact fully paid up members of this fascist political movement. A fact we learnt from records held on file at the Kew Public Record Office, which having been kept secret for 60 years were released for public viewing in 2005.

But going back to the 1930s, at this time the vicar was the head of the old Church School, a post he held since he took over as Vicar of Rustington in 1908, and it would appear that he was trying to influence the children into understanding and believing that Hitler was trying to do what he could to make Europe a much better place and he should be admired and respected as a wonderful leader.

It was around this time, in 1935, my grandfather advised my parents to send me to school in East Street, Littlehampton (now the Flintstone Centre) rather than being sent to the Rustington Church School.

In 1934, Mr Albert Pickup was appointed the new headmaster at the school. He had three teachers/teaching assistants under him who were Miss Iris Williams, Miss Gooch and Miss Ford. A year later, the Church School was no longer to be known as such and it became the Rustington Primary School.

Prior to his appointment, and whilst Mr Pickup was getting

to grips with being headmaster at the little Church School, he became somewhat harassed and frustrated by Vicar Crosland coming into the school to give lectures to the pupils and even more so when he discovered the subjects of these lectures. Despite Mr Pickup's concerns, these lectures continued.

East Street School, Littlehampton. (98)

So it was not really surprising when four men came into the school early in 1938 wearing black shirts to talk to the older boys, much to the disgust of the teachers. Two of the men were strangers to the pupils and teachers. However, the other two were the vicar's son, John Sidney Crosland, and the other William Joyce. It seems the objective was to introduce the young minds and bodies to a militaristic routine at an early age, in order to prepare them for the struggle for power in the war which was to come. The four men let it be known that they were driving to Bognor afterwards to attend one of Oswald Mosley's meetings.

The very next day, a closely typed letter of some four pages was taken to the three lady teachers, which in part praised Hitler and all he stood for in hoping to achieve to make a better Europe. The teachers were asked to sign the letter, but they refused. Miss Williams told me, *"As far as she was concerned, she refused to be bullied into signing anything."* Apparently, a copy of the letter was taken into Mr Pickup, but there is no record of what he did about it. He had become very worried about this situation at the little school dominated by the vicar and was most anxious to get started at the new school when it was ready.

I was told some years later about what was going on at the school, from about 1936 until the school was moved to North Lane in 1939, by two of the teachers independently. Miss Iris Williams was one and I was asked by the other if she could remain anonymous. Miss Williams asked me to go and visit her at her home when I was writing the book *In Times of War*, to say what had been going on in these pre-war years.

My grandfather was also apparently getting very worried, as he said, *"Every time he went to The Vicarage, 'Blackshirt' meetings were taking place and that William Joyce actually stayed there more times than I've had hot dinners."*

William Joyce (aka Lord Haw Haw). (99)

On advice, grandfather decided to go up to London to consult with certain barristers regarding what he knew to be going on at The Vicarage in Rustington and was advised to take his sons away from the choir as soon as possible, which he promptly did.

Grandfather's last bill to the vicar, was as follows:

Expenditure 1st January – 31st December 1939

Paid to Mr George Richard Sopp

To Repairs to Church Tower etc.	£ 3 11s 2d
To Work in Churchyard and clearing Burial Ground	
In in Worthing Road	£ 9 8s 2d
To Blacking out the Church and the necessary materials	
	£ 2 5s 1d
	£15 4s 5d

And with that he ceased all connection with the church.

The new modern school for both infants and primary children was being built in North Lane where fields of broad beans once grew. It was almost completed by the July of 1939 and was officially opened on 11th September 1939.

In October 1939, J Louis Crosland wrote in the Parish Magazine, *"At a special meeting of the Church Council, it was resolved to abandon our proposed Christmas Fayre this year on account of the war and the difficulty in getting about during the 'Blackout'... On or after the first Sunday in October, Evensong will be at 3 o'clock instead of 6.30p.m. until further notice, on this Sunday special forms of intercession will be used in church for the help and guidance of God in this time of trouble. I trust that you will not only take part in these services, but will also continue to pray during the national emergency, that the issues of this war will be over-ruled for the glory of God, and the establishment of freedom, justice and peace throughout the world."*

(Authors' comment – strangely worded prayer at the end of the paragraph.)

Meanwhile, the new school was up and running, Miss Williams produced plays for the children to perform during the year. One they performed to the Canadian soldiers stationed at the Lido. However, detectives following information received were now visiting the headmaster, teachers and parents of the schoolchildren to enquire as to what extent indoctrination was affecting their children.

Left: Rustington Church School c. 1908. (100)

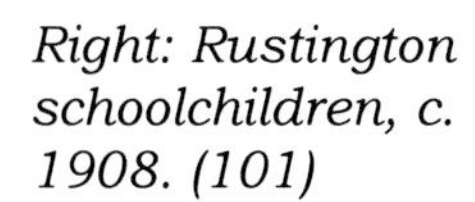

Right: Rustington schoolchildren, c. 1908. (101)

Mr Pickup, who had done his very best to protect the children from the outside influences to which they were being subjected, found that his own health started to deteriorate. One wonders whether he was coerced into signing that incriminating letter. In October 1940, Mr Pickup took a month's sick leave before returning for the remainder of the school term. He died very suddenly and unexpectedly on January 1st 1941.

Pupils at the Rustington School in 1938-9 prior to the new school being opened. (102)

The entrance to the new school in North Lane, 1939. (103)

Classrooms in the new school in 1939. (104)

Following these interviews and from other information, which we will disclose later, the vicar's son, John Sidney Crosland, who had become, in the spring of 1940, Oswald Mosley's Regional Inspector for the whole of Sussex, was interned under the Defence Regulation 18B, without trial in June 1940. In the church records it states that John Sidney Crosland had resigned his position as church warden as he had volunteered to join the navy. It also states that Mr Crosland's health had begun to fail, so he and his wife left the village to convalesce at their new private residence at The Priory in Cross-in-Hand, East Sussex. There he was to remain until his death in 1943.

Following the vicar's sudden departure the Reverend George Gordon, the Vicar of Poling, undertook to carry on the services and work of the Parish.

The Vicarage after being searched, and articles removed for evidence against John Sidney Crosland, was immediately taken over by the military. Troops from various regiments were stationed there and from June 1942 the Home Guard's headquarters were established there.

From subsequent research we have been able to ascertain more information as to what actually happened during this period, which we will now share with you.

Firstly, from information we gratefully received from Diana MD Bailey, the daughter of Commander Charles Edward Hudson RNR (Retired) OBE (mil) RD., Croix de Guerre, and Alma Violet Derrington Bell (she had been taught to sing by Elgar). The family were living at the time at 'Arnen', Limmer Lane, Felpham, near Bognor Regis.

Left: The Hudson's house in Felpham. (105)

Below left: Commander Hudson and his wife Alma. (106)

Below right: Commander Hudson. (107)

When we went to visit her at her home in Pershore, she confirmed a lot of the details we had already uncovered, and provided us with additional information for our use in this book. Diana was born on 12th June 1925, in Copenhagen where her father served as a British Consul. He was also an ex-founder member of MI6, formerly of British Naval Intelligence, a founder member of both the British Legion and the Anglo-German Fellowship. Her grandfather was the first person in the army to have been awarded the Victoria Cross in the Crimea War.

She told us that John Crosland was doing his seminary training in Chichester to become a priest when they first met. John was an enthusiastic Mosleyite who persuaded her father to join the movement in 1932. At the time her father was already in his 60s and John was only 21. Both men were particularly angry about the treatment of returning soldiers and other servicemen after the Great War, some having to stoop to selling matches on street corners in order to survive etc. There was no counselling or other help for these poor men in those days. Then as now, Britain for the British was a very strong slogan.

Diana has given us a copy of a very strong speech her father had made at the Annual Dinner of the Felpham and Middleton Branch of the British Legion, which was published in the *Bognor Regis Observer* on Wednesday February 1st 1939, the wording of which we have printed below:

"Today we are hearing the drums of war. They are beating throughout Europe. The tuck-tuck of the drum is sounding in this country. We hope that no war will come, but if it does, we know our men and women are all ready to respond, immediately, to the call of the nation, and they will fulfil those things required of them to protect their homes and country.

UP BRITAIN
STOP WAR

REMEMBER THE LAST WAR

The call to arms - Millions murdered in cold blood - Thousands maimed and blind - Millions left fatherless - The war wrecks to-day walk the gutters of Britain - Many without Pensions.

MILLIONS MADE THE SUPREME SACRIFICE TO SAVE "POOR LITTLE BELGIUM."

THE MILLIONS OF WARRIOR DEAD ARE FORGOTTEN.

YOU *are pledged to die for POLAND and other states where INTERNATIONAL FINANCE has lent MONEY.*

Who massed profits in the last war who will gain by another?

STOP THE MAD DRIVE TO WAR
MIND BRITAIN'S BUSINESS

MOSLEY SAYS PEACE

Join BRITISH UNION

30 COLESHILL ST. B'HAM.

Poster showing the reasons why so many people, including John SG Crosland, joined the British Union. (108)

We frequently hear this expression cast at our nation – 'We have become decadent and effete' – I can cast that expression back into their teeth. How can our people forget the millions of men who sacrificed their lives in the last war? Those men who today are resting under the poppies of Flanders throw to us the torch which we were to carry and to live up to for their great sacrifice."

On another occasion he declared whilst attending a British Legion dinner at the Elmer Hotel in Felpham that *"'I am carrying on the ideals of war into peace time"*.

During the 1930s, many visitors were invited to have dinner with the Hudson family in Felpham, these included Oswald Mosley, William Joyce, Jorian Jenks, Charles Henry Bentinck Budd and other leading members of the Blackshirts. Diana's mother, Alma Hudson, became the Women's District Leader for Bognor and spoke at a gathering in Slindon. Her aunt, Doreen Bell (her mother's sister), married the British Union Director of Public Relations, Archibald Findlay, who was secretary to Oswald Mosley. Doreen Bell, also a Blackshirt speaker nationally, became the movement's prospective candidate for Accrington in Lancashire. Doreen, however, did not get interned under Defence Regulation 18B. She is pictured with Oswald Mosley at one of the camps.

Doreen Bell and Archibald Findlay on their wedding day. (109)

Doreen Bell pictured immediately left of Oswald Mosley at one of the summer camps. (110)

Diana is pictured left of Oswald Mosley and Commander Charles Hudson, the person wearing the hat. (111)

Commander Charles Hudson was to eventually become the British Union Leader for Sussex and parliamentary candidate for Chichester. He was one of only nine people in the whole country, at the outbreak of the Second World War, whom Mosley nominated to act on his behalf if Mosley were to be assassinated or imprisoned. This we expect is the reason why Commander Hudson was held for a longer period of time under Defence Regulation 18B.

One amusing anecdote she told us was that when her father was a local councillor, Vice Chairman of Felpham Council, the Bognor Regis Urban District Council invited Councillor Hudson to design a new coat of arms for the town. This he duly did, and he was accorded 'a hearty vote of thanks for his valuable assistance' by the council. The arms were granted on April 10th 1935. The original coat of arms that he designed had the British Union's weekly newspaper's title 'Action' as its motto. The design was used in a wide range of council material until they realised the significance of the motto. Eventually the motto was replaced with the wording 'To Excel'. This coat of arms was adopted by the Bognor Regis Town Council shortly after its formation in 1988 and can still be seen today, minus the fascist logo, on the road signs entering the town and adorning the façade of the Bognor Regis Town Hall in Clarence Road.

(112)

(113)

Diana was one of the contributors to the Radio 4 programme *Mother was a Blackshirt*, broadcast on 4th January 2010, and also wrote an article about her memories of the Blackshirt movement in 1934 saying, *"My siblings – a sister, brother and I aged ten, nine and seven respectively, joined in the excitement. Oswald Mosley came to dinner, we painted slogans on street walls, raised our arms in Nazi salute, shouted PJ (perish the Jews), and sang* Giovinezza *– an Italian Fascist song."*

Diana also remembers meeting John's mother Constance, who she said walked with a noticeable limp and waving her crutch around in the air, at The Priory in Cross-in-Hand and told us that she was really frightened of Constance as she had such a stern demeanour.

When war came in 1939, Diana told us that her father and John Crosland manned, with a couple of others, a small boat on the Thames minesweeping and that she had been at the Sion Convent School in Worthing, but was moved to a convent in Haywards Heath, with monastic nuns, called The Priory, a very substantial property with a monastery, a school and forty acres of woodland. The school was of a high international and intellectual level. It was here that Diana saw in a newspaper that a naval officer's wife from Felpham had been interned on 30th May 1940. She immediately realised who it was, screwed up the paper and threw it in the waste paper bin. Later that afternoon, the headmistress, 'Chere Mere', who was in her late twenties... with an uncanny understanding of teenage girls... called Diana into her office to tell her the devastating news about her mother. Chere Mere told her that no one outside the room would find out about what had happened. Her father told her that he was going to make the birthday cake for her so that everything would look as normal at school, which he did. Just a day before her birthday on 11th June 1940, her father was also interned.

She said: *"My father spent three and a half years on the Isle of Man, whilst my mother had nine months in Holloway, with neither of them ever being charged. In the meantime we children had stones thrown at us and felt orphaned. 1944 came; I joined the WRNS at age seventeen, and was posted to Mountbatten's Headquarters in Ceylon, followed by Singapore. One day I saw a film of Richard Dimbleby entering the Belsen camp. The profound guilt I felt was beyond comprehension, and altered my trajectory for the rest of my life."* (*University*, 2013)

Diana also mentioned that whilst in detention on the Isle of Man, John Crosland and her father shared their own house with two German prisoners of war as servants. They were obviously well thought of to be given this privilege.

Could it be that the former founder member of MI6, Commander Charles Hudson, who became camp leader in Huyton, was sent into the British Union as an infiltrator to the movement by MI5? Both her sister Elizabeth and brother Richard were of the opinion that Commander Hudson may have been an MI5 infiltrator but Diana has refuted this following her extensive enquiries into the matter.

In a letter Diana wrote to us she said that John Crosland went on to become a public figure of much local distinction. For nearly 49 years he occupied positions on his local council, eventually leading the council. He never married but was always very fond of her elder sister. Diana used to stay with him for a weekend once a year, at The Green Farm, Froxfield Green, Petersfield, until he died in 1995. She said she always viewed him as one of the most upright and honourable men she had ever known. John also became godfather to Elizabeth's son, Edward McMillan Scott, who became a Vice President of the European Union.

We now move onto the information gathered by the Home Office on JSG Crosland's file. His case number was No. 840533. (*The National Archives*, 1940-1945)

A picture of Mary with John Sidney George Crosland's file at the National Archives at Kew. (114)

When the order came for John Sidney Crosland to be detained, officers were sent to The Vicarage at Rustington, but on their arrival the Rev. Crosland informed them that his son was at a house known as 'Brook Lyn', Cross-in-Hand in East Sussex, with 16 acres of land. He had contracted to buy this property so that he could live there with his parents to farm the land. It was here in Cross-in-Hand that John Sidney George Crosland was detained on 4th June 1940. JSG had only been at the farm for about a week to ten days after having moved from Jorian Jenks's farm in Forest Row. (A copy of this map is in the appendix.) He was to be detained at HM Prison in Huyton, Liverpool until 31st July 1940.

The statement against John Sidney George Crosland, dated 26th August 1940, was as follows:

"This man is the son of the Vicar of Rustington and has been an active member of the Fascist party since 1932. His father was also a Fascist and gave evidence on behalf of Mosley when the latter was charged with riot after disturbances at a Fascist meeting in Worthing in 1934. The son was County Volunteer Transport Organiser and Regional Inspector. In the

latter capacity, he was one of the most important, if not the most important official of the B.U. in Sussex. He was indefatigable in his activities, and a search of the property of the other officials of the Party in Sussex shows almost invariably quantities of correspondence with CROSLAND upon all sorts of fascist activities right up to the date of his arrest. On 23rd May after Mosley's arrest, he sent out the letter to District Leaders urging them to continue their functions within the limits of the law and we have also a letter dated 31st May 1940 from one George LING acknowledging a letter from CROSLAND and offering to take over a District leadership.

CROSLAND organised meetings in the district, and in some cases was the speaker, as an example of which he wrote on 15th April, 1940 to JEEVES, the D/L of Brighton asking him to arrange for a Hall for 1st June 1940. Again on the same date he wrote to District Leaders urging the necessity of increasing the sale of 'Action' as it is the best medium of propaganda that our movement possesses.

The Chief Constable of West Sussex further reports that CROSLAND's pro-Nazi views were well known and that he was friendly with the leaders of the movement, including William JOYCE (Lord Haw-Haw) who on occasions stayed at the Rectory. He has been to Germany on several occasions and among his property was found a letter from the DEUTSCHE FICHTE BUND, Hamburg, and on another a man named Heinrig WALZ of 30th June 1938, in reply to a request of CROSLAND's giving directions to write to the National Socialist Party in Munich. In April of this year he moved to the house of Jorian JENKS from which he carried on his Fascist activities, using the name of GEORGE, under which his mother wrote him letters.

Among his property was found:-

i. Two photographs of Hitler

ii. Complete Fascist uniform

iii. *Nazi Badge*

iv. *Large quantity of Fascist literature.*

v. *Hand drawn map of East Sussex (where recent bombing raids have taken place).* (See below.)

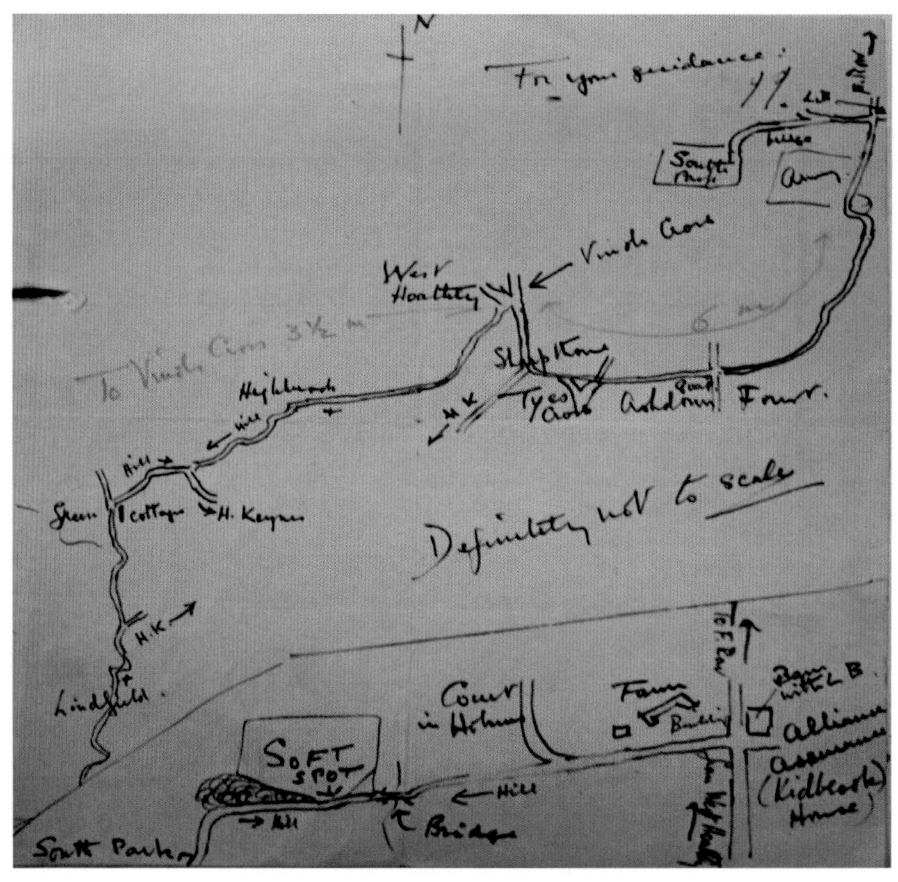

(115)

The Committee is asked to consider this case in conjunction with the 'General Report on Fascist Activities in West Sussex' which is sent herewith.

The Chief Constable of West Sussex regards CROSLAND as a very dangerous person."

A printed armband as worn by members of the B.U.F. (116)

B.U.F. bullion wire cap badge. (117)

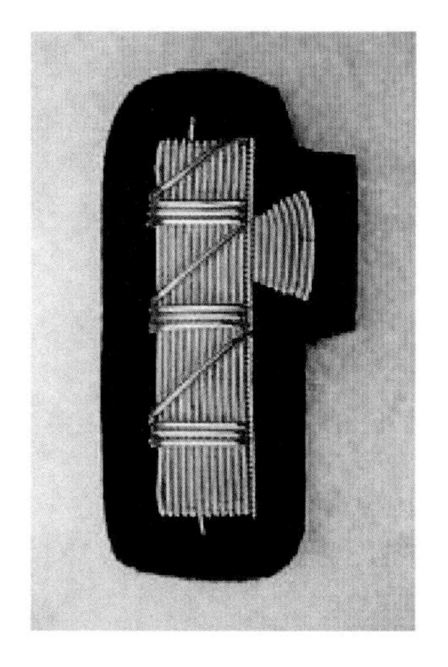

GENERAL REPORT OF FASCIST ACTIVITIES IN WEST SUSSEX

Of all the counties in the South of England Sussex is the most important from the Fascist point of view. Throughout the county the movement was well organised, led by enthusiastic persons and persistently active until the time the principal members were arrested. In Sussex itself, the movement was strongest in West Sussex, although there were numbers of other districts with strong active memberships, such as Hastings and Brighton.

Commander HUDSON whose detention the committee has decided must be continued was the leading man in West Sussex, although he was energetically supported by a number of able subordinates. Working in close co-operation with him as Regional Inspector of the whole of Sussex was J.S.G. Crosland whose case is one of those now sent to the Committee.

We are fortunate in being able to place before the Committee some idea of the extent of the organisation by piecing together facts found in documents in the possession of some of the Sussex Officials.

In a letter from CROSLAND to JEEVES, the District Leader of Brighton of 12th March 1940, the names of the District and Sub-District Leaders are given.

These include:-

Chichester Division D/L Commander – C.E. HUDSON

Worthing & Horsham Division D/L – L LION

S/D/L Horsham – A. NIGHTINGALE

That letter also gives Jorian JENKS as Prospective Candidate for the Worthing and Horsham Division. The case of LION is one of those sent herewith to the Committee; those of NIGHTINGALE and JENKS were sent separately some time ago because the Committee thought them urgent cases. In both these latter cases, the Committee have recommended release, but we are communicating further with them in a separate letter drawing attention to certain aspects of these cases and the general local position.

There were also a sub-District of Petworth with BRYANT and COX as the officials.

We are also able to assist the committee by giving them some idea of the numbers of members. The Chief Constable estimated the number of adherents in Bognor as about 300. Upon the search of Commander HUDSON's premises there were found lists of names, addresses and dates of enrolment of members in his district, which included Bognor and Chichester, and these total 250-300. These lists were apparently kept up to date because there are certain notes against some of the names including, for example, against one of the 'Letter of resignation 27.4.40'. Worthing membership was estimated to be about 60, and in a letter from NIGHTINGALE, the Leader of the Sub-District of Horsham dated 7th February 1940 some indication of the strength of the movement in that area is given by the fact that he writes: - "We hope to get a coach-load for Bognor on the 18th as some of our members have not heard or seen our Leader."

As to the amount of activity, we know that the area was of sufficient importance for Mosley himself to speak at four meetings in recent times, the last being in February of this year at the Theatre Royal Bognor, and the Chief Constable reports that there were numerous parades and meetings, both open-air and indoor.

We have also the 'Formation Monthly Report' prepared by Commander HUDSON for April 1940 which discloses among other things that in March five indoor meetings were held, three 'Sales Pitches' were regularly covered and 800 leaflets distributed in addition to the enrolment of 1 recruit. This, of course, only refers to Bognor and Chichester District.

The internment of the persons whose cases have come before the Committee or whose cases are sent herewith has done much to stamp out Fascist activity in West Sussex, but it is evident that there are still fascist sympathisers and that the return of any of their Leaders might well cause a recrudescence of their activities. In his report of 17th August 1940 the Security Liaison Officer reports that he has just had to recommend an internment order against another man,

Robert TRAINI, who was an associate of many of the persons from this district already interned and that on his arrest TRAINI said, "The Dirty Dogs. All I can say is 'God help them the day Mosley gets into power'." The security officer also states that a few instances have been reported of Fascist sympathisers indulging in defeatist talk, but he is able to state that they have made no impression on their hearers who report the matter to the Police, and as a result, within recent times, several members of the party have been interned or restricted.

One further passage from this officer's report may assist the Committee in gauging the extent of the activities of the party. He reports "The Chief Constable of West Sussex has commented on the number of Bank employees at Horsham who were members of the B.U.F. The manager of the Midland Bank was interned. Two employees of the National and Provincial Bank prominent members have severed their connection with the Party. They are, however, reported to be sympathetic, but it is not proposed to take any action against them for the present... It is, however, curious that in a small town like Horsham, the B.U.F. should find so many adherents among Bank employees.

The Chief Constable further requested on 21.8.40 that "there still remains a small group of active Fascists who are the subject of Police enquiry and observation" and that the release of any of the officials would cause a public scandal and lead to a renewal of Fascist propaganda.

At this time JSG Crosland had already been moved to 1759, Room B, POW Camp No. 7 in Ascot, Berkshire. He was here from 31st July 1940 to February 1941. Whilst at this camp, JSG Crosland appealed against his internment on 10th September 1940. Following this letter a meeting was held at the Berystede Hotel, in Ascot on 7th October 1940.

He was examined by the Home Office Advisory Committee and the transcript covers seventeen pages so we'll share with you just some of the more important points.

John SG Crosland confirmed that he had been a West Sussex County Councillor for 3½ years, serving on several committees, and a Rustington Parish Councillor for 4 years, a Churchwarden for 5 years, and between 1935 and 1938 a member of the Special Constabulary. He also added that he only resigned from this as he had become chief warden of the Rustington ARP Services. He had also joined the British Red Cross in April 1937 and went to the Home Office Anti-Gas School at Fairfield, qualifying for a First Class Instructor's Certificate before being appointed the Red Cross Anti-gas Officer for West Sussex. This involved lecturing and examining in many parts of the country on gas.

In August 1939, he volunteered for the River Emergency Service and became Deputy Master of the motor yacht 'Winona' stationed at Greenhithe on the River Thames. However, owing to haemorrhoids, he had to resign from this post.

Following this, John Crosland went to stay on Jorian Jenks's farm at Forest Row for about a month between the end of April 1940 and the end of May 1940 before negotiating the purchase of the poultry farm at Cross-in-Hand where he was duly arrested. Jenks drew a map of the location so that JSG could find it.

JSG Crosland joined the British Union on 12th December 1932 after reading Oswald Mosley's book *Greater Britain.* The part he says he was really interested in was the Imperial Policy of Empire Trade. It was also in late 1932 that he bought some land, being part of Micklepage Farm and part of Cooks Farm, in Nuthurst, near Horsham. He wanted to take up farming, but the family trustees would not agree to the money being put up for the farm. JSG held the land for a while before selling it.

In July 1933, he opened a branch in Littlehampton, becoming District Leader; this was splitting the Worthing and Littlehampton organisations into two branches. In

1935, John Crosland retired and went non-active because he had an argument about the types of people being recruited into the movement; he told the committee that there was a lot of trouble in the neighbourhood at the time and he did not care for their characters and their records, thinking them unsavoury. He goes on later to say it was more the queer goings on at the local headquarters in Worthing – that is, officials going off with other people's wives.

JSG says that he remained non-active until early 1939, when he wrote for some tickets for a meeting that Oswald Mosley was holding in Horsham in February 1939. He was then asked by Headquarters if he would take on the job of County Transport Organiser for Sussex. It wasn't until the first week of August that JSG became the Regional Inspector for the whole of Sussex. JSG admits to doing a certain amount of speaking in the summer of 1939, including both Chichester and Horsham, and making appeals for funds for the organisation.

When JSG Crosland was asked what was meant by the letter he had written to the District Leaders on 15th April 1940, urging the necessity of increasing the sale of *Action* as it is the best medium of propaganda the movement possesses, he replied that the British Union's view was that of 'a peace by negotiation'. What JSG had hoped at the beginning of the war, was that we could have peace where Germany would have cleared out of Poland, that part of Poland which was Polish. He said he realised that this would not be possible when the Germans started pressing to the west and when France was getting pressed.

It was mentioned at the hearing that the committee had received character witnesses from the following people on behalf of JSG Crosland:

Mr Arthur Furneaux of Palm Cottage, Rustington; Miss Cecilia Langfield (a retired schoolmistress) of 67c South Terrace, Littlehampton; Mr Edward Hopper of Mentone,

Rustington; Miss EH Atkinson of West Preston, Rustington; and finally Mr TA Healey (the organist and choirmaster of Rustington Church) of 1 Tennyson Avenue, Rustington.

Another area the committee and the Home Office were especially keen to find out more about was his association with William Joyce; JSG consistently says that William Joyce only stayed once at The Vicarage and that was in 1934. This is contrary to what we have written earlier.

There is a statement on the JSG Crosland file from a Violet Enid Watts of No.4 New Albert Road, Rustington, a 19-year-old housemaid working at The Vicarage. The statement reads:

I reside with my mother at No. 4 New Albert Road, Rustington. At the moment I am unemployed.

During 1936, when I was 15 years of age I was employed by Mrs Constance Crosland at 'The Vicarage', Rustington as a daily help. I left this employment at the end of 1936 owing to my mother's ill health.

In May 1939 I again obtained employment with Mrs Crosland as a daily help. In August 1939, this was before the war; Mrs Crosland told me that William Joyce was a great friend of theirs in particular old Mr Crosland who was the vicar of Rustington. She told me Joyce had stayed in Room No 6 during the previous summer which was 1938; she also said he had a scar on his face. I was told by Mrs Crosland not to believe things that were being said about Joyce as he was a very nice man and was trained at the London University and was very high class, he was an Englishman but preferred to be in Germany with the German people. Mrs Crosland said when Joyce left the Vicarage he gave her a present of a bed-side lamp.

After the war had broken out Mrs Crosland asked me if I listened to the German propaganda station, I said, "Yes", she then said, "Do you know who it is?", I replied, " We all think it is Baille Stewart", she said, "You are wrong, I will tell you one day". Later Mrs Crosland said, "Who does your mother think it is?" I said, "The same man, Stewart", she then said, "You are not right, it is William Joyce". Mrs Crosland told me we did not publish the truth and not to believe anything against Joyce.

I have never seen William Joyce in person during my employment at the Vicarage, visitors did come but Mrs Crosland would not let me get near the door, I cannot say who they were.

I saw Sydney Crosland several times whilst he was living at the Vicarage, at the outbreak of war he went away and Mrs Crosland told me he was on a boat with the Thames Police.

Room 6 was usually locked and I went in to clean it out twice a week, there was only a bedroom suite in this room, nothing was lying about and I naturally thought it was empty.

The above statement has been read over to me and it is true.

Signed: - V. Watts

We find it a little surprising that neither Reverend James Crosland nor his wife Constance Humphrey Crosland were interned, given their sympathies at the time and the amount of documents and other items relating to the movement having been found by the constabulary at The Vicarage.

It was John SG Crosland's alleged association with William Joyce which appears to have been the reason for his extended internment up until his release from Peveril Internment Camp on the Isle of Man on 21st August 1941. He had moved from Ascot to the Isle of Man in February 1941. If it hadn't been for this association, we believe from the correspondence we have read that John Crosland would have been released earlier, as the Home Office appeared to believe John to be of lower intelligence and perhaps being unaware of the consequences of his actions on behalf of the movement.

Later questioning involved items found at The Vicarage and the farm and his trips to Germany. There were some 93 articles removed from The Vicarage and a further 20 from the farm. They had called the farm 'High Hedges' rather than 'Brook Lyn'; we do not know the reason for the change. (See Appendix 3 for full list. See if you can find the error on the list – answer after Acknowledgements.)

Included in the items removed were:

- 2 photographs of Hitler, on the reverse of one of the pictures is written: *"Dear Sidney, I hope you will enjoy this picture of your beloved Hitler."* And the other has *"With best wishes from Germany"* written on the back.

- A typewritten letter from Deutscher Fichter-Bund e.D., Hamburg, 36, with stamp and swastika badge and typed slip. This contains an offer to send leaflets for distribution – note that German leaflets were found at the 'Black Rabbit', Arundel, bearing the same address.

- Two copies of *On National Socialism and World Relations* by Adolph Hitler bearing the same stamp as above.

- Two West Sussex CC electioneering addresses by Crosland with German writing on the back.

- Typewritten letter from Heinz Walz of 10, Lovaine Place, Newcastle. This tells Crosland to write to the National Socialist Party at Munich.

- A typewritten letter in German to Miss Ruth Dalitz, The Vicarage, Rustington from *Die Deutsche Arbeitsfront.*

- Notes, visiting cards, German wavelengths giving the wavelengths and times of foreign broadcasts, and fascist tie pins.

- Membership cards; car pennant with fascist badge

> thereon; leather belt with fascist buckle; one cap with fascist badge thereon; two fascist flags with badge thereon; three copies of poster 'Mosley's meeting at Bognor Regis, 18th February, 1940'; rubber whip; fascist motor car flag. Lots of fascist literature.

Also on the list was correspondence with the AA for travelling with a motor car in Germany – dated late August, 1939! When questioned at the hearing, he said he was planning a proposed tour of Germany and Belgium. He said he cancelled the trip as war looked imminent.

Here below is a copy of the letter to the insurance company:

The Vicarage,
Rustington,
Nr Littlehampton.
Sussex.

22nd August, 1939.
General Accident Fire & Life Association,
Chapel Road, Worthing, Sussex
Dear Sir,

Further with reference to my previous letter regarding my proposed tour in Germany and Belgium, I shall be leaving by the night boat from Dover to Ostend on Friday 1st September, next, I should be glad if you will kindly hold me covered for one month's touring in these countries.

I have to inform you that there will be two drivers, myself and Commander Hudson, R.N. Ret'd of 'Arnen', Limmer Lane, Felpham, near Bognor-Regis, Sussex, but I understand my Policy covers any number of qualified drivers.

Yours faithfully,

Councillor J. Sidney Crosland C.C.

He was not pushed on this, but given that his family's supposed friend William Joyce had not long since left the country with his family to Germany, we are surprised that this element was not looked into further. Especially as 1st September 1939 was the day Germany invaded Poland, with France and England declaring war on Germany just two days later.

The questions that remain unanswered and we'll leave for the readers to contemplate are:

1) Was it really for a holiday? They had previously both been on holiday to Germany and visited one of the Nuremburg rallies.

2) Given that William Joyce, a supposed friend of the family, had recently left England bound for Germany, were John SG Crosland and Commander CE Hudson planning to also move out to Germany?

3) Who else would be going with them, noting that Commander Hudson was married with three teenage children?

Now, one of the other items used in the evidence against JSG Crosland was a letter emanating from The Vicarage in 1936. The letter was handed in to the police on 31st May 1940 by Miss Boniface of 10, Woodlands Road, Littlehampton. Miss Boniface had, for many years, been headmistress of East Street Girls', Littlehampton, and of recent years had been the district representative to the County Education Board.

In this capacity she was visited by many teachers for advice and opinion. During 1936 a teacher attached to Rustington Council School called on her and said that the headmaster of the school, a Mr Pickup, had been circulating a letter to the staff and asking them to sign it. On being given a rough outline of the contents of the letter, Miss Boniface asked the teacher to take a copy and let her have a copy.

On reading the letter, Miss Boniface told the teacher that on no account should the staff give their signatures to such a document.

Miss Boniface presentation in 1939. (118)

A copy of the letter to Adolf Hitler is seen below:

April 1936

Vicarage,
Rustington.

Herr Reichskanzler Adolf Hitler.

In order that you may be able to fully understand the attitude of the British people towards the proposals put forward by the German Government, we the undersigned take this opportunity as representative of public opinion, to write and express our full approval of the proposals, and also our deep sympathy and understanding for the German people in their sincere effort to bring a lasting peace to the disturbed and troubled continent of Europe.

We feel that the proposals contain in themselves the

essence of a plan which could bring a new order of civilization undreamt of in the annals of history and which would once and for all establish the peace of Europe on a solid and lasting foundation.

We sympathise with the German nation in their struggle for equal status with the other great nations of Europe, and we realise that a country with so high a culture, which has contributed so much in the field of music, science, and art, should find a worthy and honoured place in the community of nations. We realise the work that your Excellency has done for Germany in particular, and for Europe as a whole is driving the menace of Communism from our midst, and we desire above all a friendship with Germany and the German people. We firmly reject the proposed Staff talks as monstrous, they are entirely out of sympathy with the feelings of the British nation, and we accord our warmest approval action of the German Government in their re-militarisation of the Rhine zone as a counter measure to the Franco-Soviet Pact.

We sincerely trust that this letter may reach your Excellency safely and that it will give you an idea of the opinion of the British people.

It is not really surprising that Mr Pickup's health started to deteriorate shortly after JSG Crosland's internment and the amount of questioning he would have been subjected to.

Following letters from his solicitors and both his father and his mother, JSG Crosland's case was being considered by the Home Office in early 1941, whilst he was being detained on the Isle of Man. However, on 6th March 1941, a letter was written to Mr and Mrs Crosland informing them the advisory committee who had been examining his case told them that they had given JSG Crosland every opportunity to clear up any matters which appeared to be to his prejudice, and that a report had been submitted to the Secretary of State. On reconsidering the whole matter the Secretary of State decided that the detention order ought to be maintained on him.

This must have been very hard on his parents, especially as a number of detainees had already been released by this date.

On 14th March 1941, both the Rev. James Louis Crosland and his wife Constance Humphrey Crosland wrote separate letters to the Under Secretary of State at the Home Office in London from their home at The Priory in Cross-in-Hand in Sussex. The contents of both letters are here below starting with the one from his mother:

We have received your letter of 6th inst. and my husband & I are heartbroken with its contents; for we know that our son has never done or said anything against his Country or the State, if he had done so we should not worry over his detention – He was chief A.R.P. instructor from 37, teaching his fellow countrymen what to do in time of war or if there were an invasion, he has given hundreds and hundreds of lectures on this – he has also been a hard working member of the B.R.C.S. since 36: He was made 'Chief Air Raid Warden' by the parishioners where my husband was the Vicar – I do not think he would have worked and carried out all these activities had he been against his Country – believe me, he has worked hard for it – He worked right up to the outbreak of war when he volunteered his services to the Country on patrolling the Thames Waters night & day until his health gave way.

My husband has owing to ill health retired & we have recently come here to live right out in the country on sixteen acres of farmland.

We beg of you to ask the Secretary of State if he would release him on the following condition, that he remains entirely on his sixteen acres of farm land and cultivates it with food stuffs, and never goes outside the bounds until the war is ended, and that the police may come when they like to see this condition is carried out until the war is ended.

Please I beg of you again to ask the Secretary of State if he will give this his consideration.

Our son's detention is causing my husband and me, in the remaining years of our old age great misery and unhappiness. I do beseech you to see the Secretary of State and ask him if he will agree to this.

Your obedient servant
(Mrs) C.H. Crosland

Dear Sir,

No. 840533 John S. G. Crosland.

I am in receipt of your letter dated 6th inst. which has caused me much sorrow and distress. I am an old man in failing health and have been obliged to retire from my living on account of a weak heart. I have been nearly 50 years in Holy Orders, and therefore have had wide experience in the affairs of Church and State. Experience has taught me one thing in particular that no man can hold any public position of importance without coming in contact with a certain class of people who through jealousy propagate lies about one's character and purity of intention.

Now I have reason to believe that my son who holds a public position on the West Sussex County Council is undergoing that bitter experience of false friends.

You say in your letter that, "The Advisory Committee who examined his case gave him every opportunity to clear up any matters which appeared to be to his prejudice".

My wide experience in life has taught me this fact – no accused person is able to defend himself adequately in a trial against lies which are in circulation about him. He may deny them, but that is not enough. He ought to explain how those lies were started and no accused person can do that without considerable thought. Under such circumstances he requires an advocate to plead for him. Even Ministers of the Crown in Parliament rarely answer a question without notice having first been given.

But I appeal on higher reasons than that. I put it to you. Here am I an old man broken in health physically incapable of looking after my son's farm of 16 acres, would it not be more advantageous to the State and welfare of our country's need in this time of great danger to release him so that he could do something towards the production of food, provided that he abstained from all politics during the war and that he was under the supervision of the East Sussex Police?

If I thought for one moment that my son was disloyal to his country I would not have written this letter nor would I plead for his freedom.

Will you kindly give him the chance?

For man looks on the outward appearance, but God looks on the heart. Man considers the actions, but God weighs the intentions.

Believe me,

Yours very faithfully,
J Louis Crosland.

They had to wait another five months before hearing some good news in August 1941.

On 22nd July 1941, the Home Office wrote to the Commandant of the Peveril Internment Camp at Peel on the Isle of Man, saying the Secretary of State has decided to review his case and the Under Secretary would like to be furnished with a report on the conduct and character of John SG Crosland while in detention, with special references to loyalties and associations.

The reply was written on 30th July 1941 by a Senior Intelligence Officer at Peveril Internment Camp. It basically stated that Crosland appeared to have considerably modified his BU views and to have developed a democratic outlook – this was confirmed to them by his refusal when at Huyton to sign any allegiance to the BU. He at the time of the reply was residing in what was known as a non-political house, the inmates of which were his associates and it is believed that he was serious in not desiring to be associated with any political movement in the camp and that he could be considered loyal.

It was on 21st August 1941 that his parents' wishes were granted by the secretary of State. The suspension read as follows:

DEFENCE (GENERAL) REGULATIONS, 1939

SUSPENSION OF OPERATION OF DETENTION ORDER.

WHEREAS, in pursuance of the powers conferred on him by Regulation 18B (1A) of the Defence (General) Regulations, 1939, the Secretary of State directed, by Order dated the 30th May, 1940 that

John Sidney George CROSLAND

be detained.

NOW, in pursuance of the powers confirmed on me by Regulation 18B (2) of the aforesaid Regulations, I direct, by this my order, that the operation of the aforesaid order be suspended subject to the conditions as follows:-

that the above mentioned

John Sidney George CROSLAND

1. *Shall at once notify in person to the officer serving this order the address of the residence to which he is proceeding;*

2. *Shall, within twenty-four hours of arrival at the said address, notify in person to the officer in charge at the nearest police station and inform him of the address of his residence;*

3. *Shall not change his residence from one place in the United kingdom to another place in the United Kingdom*

unless he has notified in person to the officer in charge of the police station to whom he last notified the address of his residence, particulars as to the date of the proposed residence and as to the place at which he proposes to reside immediately after the change; and if a change of residence involves his removal from one police district to another, he shall, within twenty-four hours of his arrival at the address of the new residence, notify his arrival in person to the officer in charge of the nearest police station;

4. *Shall in person notify his movements monthly to the officer in charge of the police station to whom he last notified the address of his residence, except in as far as maybe otherwise permitted by the Chief Officer of Police of the district in which the police station is situated.*

The document was signed by one of his Majesty's Principal Secretaries of State on 21st August 1941 and underneath it had the wording:

Under Defence Regulation 18B a person in whose case the Secretary of State has directed that the operations of the Detention Order be suspended subject to conditions has the right to make objections in respect of any such conditions to an advisory committee. Any such objections should be addressed to the Secretary, Home Office Advisory Committee, 6 Burlington Gardens, London, W. 1.

So it was that under military escort Crosland arrived at Liverpool Police Station from the Peveril Internment Camp at 17.35 hours on 29th August 1941, where he was served with his Suspension Order. JSG Crosland let them know that the address he was proceeding to was 'The Priory', Cross-in-Hand, Uckfield, Sussex.

Following his release, John SG Crosland went to the The Priory, where he was to farm about 30 acres of arable land.

The Chief Constable of East Sussex reported, on 17th May

1942, to the Home Office, that he was working extremely hard and seems to have put his heart and soul into the work he has undertaken and suggested that consideration be given to the question of revoking the restriction order. The Home Office agreed and the restrictions were lifted by the Revocation Order dated 12th June 1942.

James Louis Crosland died the following year and his wife Constance died in 1949. Following the death of his mother, John Sidney George Crosland moved to another farm at Froxfield Green, near Petersfield, where he stayed for the rest of his life. He became very involved with the local councils there until his death in 1995.

Where John Sidney George Crosland lived up until his death in 1995. (119)

We have included a letter we have been given, typed by John Crosland a year before his death, on 26th September 1994. He was replying to a kind and thought-provoking letter from Diana Bailey saying, *"Yes I have already heard on the radio about these fanciful discoveries purported to have been made by 'so-called' Darwinianite maniacs whose credulity bedevils all reason. They have just added another million years or so to antiquity in an attempt to sustain substance for their theories, about which we know and can never know anything about. Really when one listens to all the rubbish put out by the 'media' to-day and the 'so-called' experts, one can only pity the fools who are taken in by such claptrap. Only the other morning I heard (again on the radio) that some Catholic Priest and a Presbyterian Minister had suggested having discussions with a new Neo-pagan Society that has been started by a group of New Era Demagogues. I cannot conceive how men of the cloth such as these Clerics cannot understand that Demogorgon, a mysterious diabolical magician first came to light about A.D. 450 and was regarded as an object of terror.*

John Crosland (right) pictured here with Father Edward Corbould, a Benedictine monk from Ampleforth College, at his home in Froxfield Green. (120)

The tragedy is that so many Priests and Religious have lost their faith either through insufficient instruction or the relentless influence of a materialistic world bent on the ruin of our Christian Civilisation.

The longer I live the more convinced I become that we are now witnessing the very early stages of the 'Abomination of

Desolation', the time when even the 'Elect' may be deceived and will fall into Apostasy.

Please do not think that I have become a Prophet of Doom, but merely a realist witnessing the disintegration of modern society.

I have great faith in the hereafter."

Meanwhile, back in Rustington, on 18th August 1940, a small 10-year-old girl was walking back from posting a letter in the post box set in the wall outside Abbotswood to her home in Ash Lane along the footpath leading to Station Road. When, suddenly, she spotted a strange metal object sticking out of the ground along the footpath. She ran home to tell her father, who was in the Home Guard at the time, who immediately contacted the Home Guard HQ. Within a very short while, everyone in the vicinity of Ash Lane had to be evacuated from their homes while the device was examined and made safe. The ten year old girl turned out to be the co-author of this book!

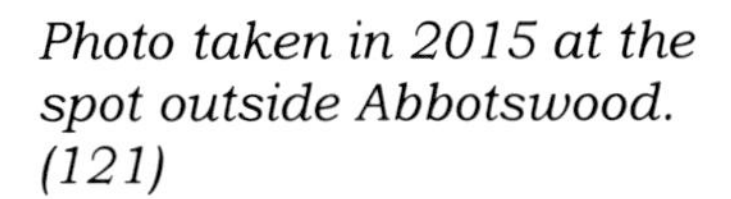

Photo taken in 2015 at the spot outside Abbotswood. (121)

Finally, we cannot leave this chapter without remarking on another recollection of Mary's.

Graeme has asked me to write and describe an incident which took place whilst Bev and I were on a three-week tour by coach, exploring Europe in September 1979. Our first ever holiday abroad!

(122)

Strange as it may seem, Bev and I were the only English people on the coach; it seems that people from all over the world would come to London to pick up this tour, so they could say they have toured England as well as the rest of Europe. It did prove to be such an interesting and amazing holiday and we made many friends.

On the German part of the tour we visited many cities and towns as well as a cruise on the Rhine. One of the German tours took us to Nuremburg city with its very beautiful flower-decked buildings and friendly people. When we went back to the coach the courier told us he would take us somewhere nearby which was called the Reichsparteitagsgelände (Reich Party Congress Grounds) for a photo opportunity. Everyone piled onto the coach and off we drove to the south-east part of Nuremburg until we found ourselves driving into an extremely vast, deserted and eerie place, with tall perimeter walls with a giant podium visible at the very far end. (Graeme has told me since that the grounds cover about 11 square kilometres of land.) I realised then that this was where six Nazi party rallies were held between 1933 and 1938. (One of which was attended by John Crosland and Commander Hudson.)

Anyway, our courier suggested that the ladies may like to each run up the many steps to the podium whilst their partners stay below to take photos of the ladies doing the typical Nazi salute when it was their turn. What great fun we all thought, although I do not think any of us knew, at the time, what this place was, or its significance, so all of us ladies lined up to take our turn to walk to the podium, having climbed dozens of steps to reach this level. When each lady left the podium, where apparently Adolf Hitler stood to give his speeches, the next in line went out to stand there and give the Nazi salute. (One has to remember, that media coverage/knowledge of the place was not as easily accessible as it is now.)

Soon it became my turn, I stepped out proudly to take my place, saw Bev waiting with the camera to take his photo, and I raised my right arm to take the Nazi salute, when suddenly everything changed. I could no longer see Bev, all that I could see were rows and rows of German troops, thousands upon thousands of them right to the back of this stadium and along each side of the walls. I could see hundreds of red flags with the swastika set in a white circle on them fluttering in the breeze, just behind I realised I was flanked by the German high command. Suddenly, I became aware of a noise penetrating the silence, at first quiet, then gradually increasing in intensity and I could make out the continuous chanting of 'Sieg Heil'; it got louder and louder until it rose to a huge crescendo, I could bear it no longer, I managed to turn around and ran down the steps until I came out of the podium and onto the vast virtually empty space, straight past poor Bev towards our coach. The courier caught up with me and made me sit by myself at the back of the coach and gave me a strong drink and left me on my own for a short while, not letting anyone else board the coach. He then returned and sat beside me and quietly said, *"I think I know what happened to you up there, I have been a courier for this company for many years and I always bring my tour guests, as I call them, here all the time on each tour and I am going to tell you in all honesty, that in all the time I have done this, you are only the second person who has had this reaction. Now, I will tell you what this lady told me, what she saw and heard. She said 'She was watching what appeared to be a Nuremburg rally and was actually beside all the German top brass and listening to a speech by Hitler, and then the Sieg Heil response which became deafening.' She then ran off the podium as you did. Is this what happened to you?"*

"Yes, exactly," I replied. *"But why did this happen?"*

"I don't know," he said, *"but this vast space has been left like this since the war, they have tried to make use of it, but nothing takes place because of the weird atmosphere, so I bring people here on every tour and wait to see if anyone should actually see and hear what you just experienced."*

(123)

I have not been able to explain it since, but whenever I see any pictures or footage of the Nuremburg rallies now it sends a shiver down my spine and takes me straight back to the experience I felt back in 1979. Graeme hopes that writing this experience down in black and white may help to remove this feeling in future. I hope he is right!

(124)

Finally, we would like finish this chapter with a couple of thought-provoking comments on these winds of change.

Firstly, that Mosley and his followers in the British Union were no more responsible for Nazi wartime concentration camps than their socialist opponents in Britain were for Stalinist death camps in Russia.

Secondly, what would the Human Rights Commission have made of the internment of so many individuals, many of whom were elderly, without charge!

THE SPECIAL WIRELESS SERVICE

Although the villagers knew very little of Crosland's situation, they would have been totally unaware of other goings-on in the village. It has only recently been unearthed that a military truck, which would have been observed by some of the residents of Rustington, was playing an important part in the build-up to D-Day.

Rustington was full of troops during World War II, from Dunkirk to the day before D-Day. They were billeted at most of the larger properties in the village, including The Vicarage (as previously mentioned), The Marigolds Hotel, The Lido, The Broadmark Hotel, Millfield Convalescent Home, Rustington House and many houses on the Sea Estate that were empty because of the war. The other large property in Rustington that was requisitioned by the Ministry of Health just two days following the declaration of war on the 3rd September 1939, was The Rustington Convalescent Home. However, it remained empty for three months. It was officially closed on 13th July 1940. All the cutlery, valuables and files were sent to Carpenters' Hall in London.

Now, the Rustington Convalescent Home was purpose built by Sir Henry Harben, Master of the Carpenters' Company in 1893. He had purchased farmland near Littlehampton and was closely involved in planning the home with the architect Frederick Wheeler. The home was opened in 1894. It was designed as a place where working men could convalesce after an illness or accident and enable them to become fully active again. It was bequeathed to the Carpenters' Company when Sir Henry died in 1911. It is still owned by the Carpenters' Company and is fully modernised, providing care for a much wider community of men and women, of all ages and from all walks of life. Fifty percent of its income comes from an endowment established by Sir Henry and by a later gift from his daughter, Mrs Mary Woodside Wharrie.

(125)

The history of the Carpenters' Company goes back over 700 years, with the first written reference being a mention of a master carpenter in the City of London records of 1271. It received its first Royal Charter in 1477.

It was originally a medieval trade guild set up to look after the welfare and interests of carpenters living and working in London.

The following information came about following a letter which had been passed to us in November 2012 by Rustington Parish Council from Andy Kyte, an avid collector and restorer of World War II military vehicles.

Andy Kyte had just acquired an extremely rare British army truck that had been used during the war by the Special Wireless Service, part of the Enigma code-breaking team at Bletchley Park. He also discovered that the truck and its crew were billeted at the 'Carpenters Arms' in Rustington prior to D-Day but could find no record of the existence of such a pub.

Special Wireless Truck and, below, the inside of the truck – photos courtesy of Andy Kyte. (126)

We were able to write and tell him that the place the Special Wireless Service called the Carpenters Arms was in fact the Rustington Convalescent Home in Sea Road.

This information enabled Andy to fill in the missing piece of the jigsaw, and in gratitude he has kindly allowed us to print his research on the origins and work of this highly secret group – The Special Wireless Service.

With secrecy paramount, the Special Wireless Service truck was constantly on the move around different locations in England prior to the D-Day invasion. One of the locations was at the Rustington Convalescent Home. The truck's role was to intercept the code and send it to Bletchley Park for it to be decoded and deciphered.

(127)

The messages were sent on to Bletchley Park.

(128)

The crew comprised six army signals personnel who would work and sleep alongside their equipment either in or under the vehicle. Conditions were harsh, with cramped conditions adding to the complexity of their role. On-board generators were carried to power the radios, receivers and additional batteries. Other than additional aerials and equipment there were no outward visible signs that the truck was in any way out of the ordinary. Due to the secrecy surrounding the Special Wireless Service, vehicles carried the markings of 402 Signals Corps rather than their real identity.

(129)

(130)

Records confirm that the vehicle went ashore on D-Day+2 and travelled across Europe, before completing its service at Nijmegen where it played a key role as part of the failed 'Operation Market Garden', operating from the grounds of a shoe factory before being withdrawn as the operation faltered.

In the build up to D-Day and with training completed, the crew found themselves billeted in Rustington to await their final orders. The officers' mess was in Xylophone House – owned by Teddy Brown, the well-known xylophonist. The working place was at Millfield House (where Millfield Overstrand Estate now is); a home for children with tuberculosis, owned and run by the Metropolitan Asylums Board, this house has now been demolished. The sleeping quarters were at the convalescent home; here they found themselves for once surrounded by luxuries many had never experienced... a bar with an abundance of alcohol, grand rooms with comfortable beds, a well-stocked kitchen and a seaside setting, all a basis for dubbing their new home 'The Carpenters Arms'.

The group, a detachment of Canadian soldiers, was under the command of a Major Rowley and Captain Gentle. Their weeks were spent completing final checks and tests of their equipment as well as the laborious task of waterproofing their vehicles in preparation for the landings.

Mewsbrook Park Lake, adjoining the convalescent home, was used as a practice location for testing their equipment, the beach opposite being mined.

Aerials were erected and radio messages were intercepted. By now air superiority was very much in the hands of the British, and Luftwaffe messages were scarce. Focus turned to troop movements and monitoring the Allies' planned deception of the real location of the invasion landing places. All radio traffic was reported back to Bletchley Park via the operators based in Rustington.

Winds of change were required. As the original date of 5th June 1944 had to be postponed because of the stormy weather, the weather forecast for the 6th was vital. Eisenhower would have faced a difficult choice if the weather forecast had been for high winds and storms. It would either mean to go ahead with the invasion and risk no improvement in the weather or put the invasion force on standby, as they had done the day before, or stand the ships, planes and soldiers down until the weather improved. Fortunately, the weather improved as per the forecast on the 6th.

So when D-Day finally arrived, messages were intercepted indicating that the enemy had been successfully deceived into thinking that the invasion fleet would land at Pas de Calais.

The Special Wireless Service vehicle boarded an American Liberty ship in Tilbury Docks, Essex, bound for Normandy. The members and vehicles of the Special Wireless Service were loaded into two landing craft from the Liberty ship. The first section ashore was the rear link section; its task was to set up a communications station working between the front line troops on the beach and Corps HQ, still on the ships, but it was pinned down soon after landing. An attempt was made to contact the Special Wireless Service ashore as it was feared that it may have been captured, in which case the codes would be compromised and the unit's purpose disclosed to the enemy. There was great relief when contact was finally made. The rest of the Special Wireless Service landed the next day.

After landing they were tasked with covering both tactical and strategic radio traffic, reporting back to XXX Corps commander, Lieutenant General Horrocks, on the enemy troops ahead of them and flanking the advance inland. Another vital role was that of overall direction finding to build up information about the order of battle of the German army in Normandy, and to locate the enemy transmitting stations, enabling artillery to target the enemy communications network and frontline forces. This work was to be done from a distance of approximately one mile from the enemy front line.

Orders came from the highest level that *"Every effort must be made to defend the Special Wireless Service and their work. At all costs they must never be compromised or captured, their task is vital to the success of this operation."*

To help with the defence of the Special Wireless Section, when a section came across a German machine gun it would make use of it to avoid the distinctive sound of the British Bren gun.

All the members of the Special Wireless Service could speak at least two languages and were the only members of the Allied forces that could if necessary transmit to the German forces in Morse code.

On 14th August 1944, the Special Wireless Service sections produced a report compiled from direction finders and wireless traffic, giving the locations of almost every important unit.

Captain FD Sherreff of 110 Special Wireless Service had a very experienced operator who, despite background noise and radio static, managed to intercept and decipher the crucial message giving the German order of battle of two German Panzer divisions, and their intentions. This message was crucial to the outcome of the battle and resulted in success for the Allies and the capture of 100,000 German prisoners.

The section was asked by General Browning to try and contact the Germans in Arnhem with a view to arranging a temporary ceasefire to allow the evacuation of wounded British and German troops. The first contact was tried by telephone. There was no answer, possibly the lines were down. Direction-finding aerial loops were then tried to find the local German army wireless transmitter, where the loudest network of enemy messages seemed to be coming from, the area round the railway station in the town of Arnhem.

A decision was taken to tell the Royal Artillery to lay down a barrage on the location of the bearings from the direction-finding transmissions. The direction-finding operators were pleased with their work, but a little prematurely as the Germans were equally efficient in taking bearings from transmitting stations, and returned the fire. The direction-finding unit were not popular with the neighbouring troops that were shelled by enemy artillery.

On 12th November 1944, General Horrocks addressed the section and observed that they were the oldest members of XXX Corps. He thanked them for their work.

On 15th November 1944, the section was moved to St. Jean, Brussels, where they were stood down. Most of the men were sent to other wireless stations.

One really sad episode is regarding the Canadians who were stationed at the various houses in the village, that following D-Day they had successfully advanced in Normandy, a lot further than expected, only for the majority to be killed by so-called friendly fire from an American bombing raid.

On 3rd September 1989, the Canadian High Commissioner came to unveil a new memorial plaque on the village war memorial to commemorate the Canadian soldiers who fell in World War II that were stationed in the area.

Following the end of the war, the Rustington Convalescent Home was de-requisitioned from military occupation on 2nd August 1946 and was re-opened to patients on 1st July 1948.

APPENDIX 1

The following is a list of the respected people in the village at that time (other family members and other residents can be seen on the 1881 census).

Hugh Penfold, a barrister at Rustington House;

Charles McLean, the innkeeper at the Windmill Inn;

Thomas Bushby, a farmer living at West Preston Manor;

Edmund Moylan, annuitant at Walnut Tree Cottage;

John Batcock, a farmer at The Thatches;

Edward Lowry, a late captain of the 81st Regiment living at Rustington Hall;

James Henson, a threshing machinist at Trafalgar House;

George Boon, a farmer at Herne Farm;

Thomas Chatfield, a wheelwright at Palm Cottage;

Charles Booker, a baker at Stonefield Bakery;

Richard Henson, a farmer at The Mathews;

Albert C Bailey, a miller/baker at Sea Mill House;

William Lawler, the headmaster at School House;

Edmund Stansfield, the vicar at The Vicarage;

Ben Chatfield, a carpenter at Box Tree Cottage;

Mary Ann Humphrey, baker and greengrocer at The Post Office in Sea Lane;

John Rogers, licensed victualler at The Lamb;

James McDonald, a pensioner of the Royal Artillery in Jessamine Cottage;

Mary Boniface, annuitant at The Elms;

Eleanor Munro, annuitant at Walnut Tree House;

John Scutt, manager of private estate at Mewsbrook House;

Dowager Lady Frances Armstrong at Seafield Court (she was the mother-in-law of Dame Nellie Melba);

George and Jeremiah Pocock (brothers), gardeners and George's son-in-law Richard Hoare, a Chelsea pensioner living at Pigeon House Farm;

John Cooter and James Humphrey were both millers at Mill Cottage and Mill House respectively.

(*1881 England Census* (database online), 2004)

APPENDIX 2

NATIONAL SOCIETY FOR WOMENS SUFFRAGE.

CENTRAL COMMITTEE.

9, BERNERS STREET,

London, W.

February 14th 1873

Sir,

We have the honour to forward to you a copy of a Petition similar in object to one which has been adopted by many important Municipal Boroughs, and to request that you will be good enough to bring the subject before the [illegible] Local Board at its next Meeting.

The object of the Bill referred to in the Petition is to obtain for those women ratepayers and owners of property who possess votes in the election of Local Boards and other local governing Bodies, the right to vote also in the election of Members of Parliament.

The matter concerns the interests of a considerable portion of the constituency which elects your Board, and we venture to hope you will regard it as a fit subject for consideration.

We have the honour to remain

your obedient servants

Caroline A. Biggs

Agnes Garrett } Hon. Secs.

APPENDIX 3

List of articles found at The Vicarage and at 'High Hedges' at Cross-in-Hand.

LIST OF ARTICLES FOUND AT THE VICARAGE, RUSTINGTON.

NO.	ARTICLE.	REMARKS.
1.	Sketch of East Sussex, in envelope.	Found in CROSLAND's bedroom (Owing to recent bombing in this area it would appear important.)
2.	Photograph of Hitler in cardboard frame.	"Dear Sidney, I hope you will enjoy this picture of your beloved Hitler, I think it's per -" written on back.
3.	Coloured photograph of Hitler.	"With best wishes from Germany" written on back.
4.	Typewritten letter from Deutscher Fichte-Bund e.D. Hamburg, 36 with stamp and Swastika Badge and typed slip.	This contains an offer to send leaflets for distribution. (Please refer to Sergt. HARMER's report dated 20/5/40, re German leaflets found at the 'Black Rabbit,' Arundel, bearing the same address.
5.	Typewritten letter from Heinz Walz of 10, Lovaine Place, Newcastle.	This tells CROSLAND to write to the National Socialist Party at Munich.
6.	Typewritten letter in German to Miss Ruth DALITZ, The Vicarage, Rustington.	From Die Deutsche Arbeitsfront.
7.	Two copies "On National Socialism and Worls Relations" by Adolph Hitler.	Bearing same stamp as referred to at No. 4.
8.	Two West Sussex C.C. electioneering addresses by CROSLAND with German writing on back.	Notes in German.
9.	Correspondence with the A.A. for travelling with motor car in Germany.	Dated August, 1939.
10.	International Certificate for motor vehicles.	Dated 11th May, 1934.
11.	Two foreign routes issued to J.S. CROSLAND by the A.A.	(1) Germany and (2) Belgium, Luxembourg, Germany, and Austria.
12.	Linen map of Germany.	German map.
13.	Linen map of Belgium.	French map.
14.	German paper street map of towns and cities.	German map.
15.	Austrian paper map.	Austrian map.
16.	Ditto of Germany,	German map.
17.	Six picture travel books of Germany.	Travellers guides.
18.	Notes, visiting cards, German wavelengths etc. Fascist tie pins.	Wavelengths and times of foreign broadcasts.
19.	20 prints and 41 negatives.	Of CROSLAND and others, views etc.

Continued:

SHEET 2.

21. Receipt Ledger.

22. Pilot's guide, English Channel, by W.E. WILSON, D.S.O., containing paper with bearing marked thereon.

23. "Mein Kampf" by Adolf Hitler. Published by HURST and BLACKWELL.

24. "My Struggle" by Adolf Hitler (Paternoster Library) with words inside on fly leaf "To Mrs CROSLAND with my best wishes, from WADIKE, Christmas 1936."

25. "Through Fascism to World Power" by Munro.

26. "Greater Britain" by MOSLEY. "J. Sidney CROSLAND" thereon.

27. "Greater Britain" by MOSLEY, Branch copy (28, High Street, Littlehampton.)

28. "Famine in England" by Viscount LYMINGTON, words on fly leaf inside "J. Sidney CROSLAND: See over all the streets the Fascist banners waving, triumphant and standards of a race re-born."

29. "Fascism" by Sir Oswald MOSLEY "100 questions asked and answered."

30. MOSLEY's "Tomorrow we live."

31. Four copies of "The British Union Quarterly" April - June, July - September, October - December, 1939 and Spring 1940.

32. Protocols of the learned Elders of Zion. Translated from the Russian of NILUS.

33. "Portrait of a Leader," by A.K. CHESTERTON.

34. "The Czech Conspiracy" by George PITT-RIVERS with the name "F. Sidney CROSLAND" written on fly leaf.

35. "Social Welfare in Italy," printed by Societa Editrice Di Novissima, Rome 1936.

36. British Union of Fascists luncheon, menu card, Criterion Restaurant March 1st 1940.

37. "Spring comes again" by Jorian JENKS.

38. Souvenir Programme, Earls Court, July, 1939.

39. "Strike Action" by W. RISDON.

40. "The truth about the slump" by A.N. FIELD, marked "F. Sidney CROSLAND."

41. "The Coming Corporate State," by A. RAVEN THOMPSON.

42. "Martin Luther and the Jews" by Bishop Martin SASSE, Eisenach.

43. "Labour Lies" pamphlet by E.G. CLARK.

44. "Mind Britain's business" by Captain R. GORDON-CANNING, M.C.

45. "Palestine; the way to Peace" No. 3, by The Arab Centre, Grand Buildings, Trafalgar Square, W.C. 2.

46. "Reply of the Arab Higher Committee for Palestine to the White Paper issued by the British Government on 17th May, 1939.

Continued:

SHEET 3.

47. "Why MOSLEY left the Labour Government" House of Commons, 28th May, 1930.

48. "Taxation and the people" by Oswald MOSLEY.

49. Pamphlet "Priests hands cut off by Reds."

50. Pamphlet "Christian Spain against Jewish Soviet" 1936 - 39.

51. Pamphlet "Cover of the American Jew."

52. Pamphlet "The chosen people" (Two copies).

53. Pamphlet "Is Lancashire doomed?"

54. "What the British Union has to offer Britain" by Major-General J.F.C. FULLER, C.B., C.B.E., D.S.O.

55. Pamphlet "Labour's peace policy through British Union eyes."

56. "Education, not conscription" by Oswald MOSLEY.

57. "Against trust and monopoly" by F.D. HILL.

58. "Political and moral aspects of the New Corporate Economy in Italy" by Societa Editrice Di Novissima, Rome (Two copies).

59. "Fascism and the working classes" (Two copies.)

60. "Why are we at war?"

61. "The Ministry for the Press and Propaganda."

62. "Italy and Abyssinia" by Societa Di Editrice, Rome.

63. "The Italo-Ethiopian dispute."

64. "Britain First" verbatim report of MOSLEY's speech at Earls Court Exhibition Hall on July 16th 1939. (2 copies.)

65. "Fair play for Italy" by H.C. HOPKINSON.

66. "Parti Social Francais" with 4 photographs of male person.

67. "German - English, English - German dictionary" marked "S. CROSLAND."

68. "Arab or Jew" by Captain R. GORDON-CANNING, M.C.

69. "The Last stronghold of Slavery" by Pro. G.C. BARAVELLI.

70. "Tomorrow we live" by MOSLEY.

71. "British Union - Constitution and rules" marked "C.V.T.O. Sussex" (2 copies.)

72. Two empty folders.

73. Blank ledger marked "British Union of Fascists, local headquarters, Broadway, 28, High Street, Littlehampton."

74. One small memo book - payments of sales - Blackshirt and literature sales.

75. Blank foolscap book.

76. Membership cards - J.S. CROSLAND, 1932, 1934, John Sidney CROSLAND, 1935, 1937, and 1938.

Continued:

SHEET NO. 4.

77. Notebook with lecture on analysis of Logic.

78. Ledger - particulars of French Social party. President of party. Lt. Col. de la ROCQUE. Deputy General. Noel OTTARE. Names of members of Executive Committee with address of Social Headquarters.

79. Folder with particulars of students courses returned to National Headquarters.

80. Notebook with written material and particulars therein.

81. Book of Fascists 'Flash' labels.

82. West Sussex County Council diary.

83. Fascist diary.

84. Membership cards - James Louis (Reverend) CROSLAND, 1933, 1934 and 1935.

85. Car pennant with Fascist badge thereon.

86. Two Fascist flags with badge thereon.

87. Pages 9 and 10 of the 'Daily Mail' 22nd April, 1939.

88. Three copies of poster "Mosley's meeting at Bognor Regis, 18th February, 1940.

89. Two 'Action' posters.

90. One cap with Fascist badge thereon.

91. One leather belt with Fascist buckle.

92. 26 copies of 'Action.'

93. One gramophone record - "The Marching song and Britain awake."

LIST OF PROPERTY FOUND AT "HIGH HEDGES" CROSS-IN-HAND, EAST SUSSEX.

1. Three letters written from the Vicarage, Rustington.

2. Correspondence relating to a yacht "Isle of Arran" (Information received shows that this yacht was sold to a firm at Chichester in 1939, believed August, for the sum of £825.)

3. Letter dated 24th April, 1939, from H.K. STEVENS, Secretary to the Director - General of the British Union.

4. Letter from George J. LING dated 31st May, 1940.

5. Correspondence:-
(a) Letter dated 30th May, 1940, to Women Blackshirts.
(b) Emergency Instructions No. 2.
(c) Speaker's Notes.

6. Postcard with "10.15 p.m. Broadcast, 6th May, Saturday," thereon.

7. Membership card, British Union - 1939. John Sidney George CROSLAND.

Continued:

SHEET 5.

8. Appointment card - Air Raid warden - issued 19/1/39 to J.S.G. CROSLAND.

9. Admission ticket - British Union second 1940 luncheon - Friday 26th April, 1940, No. 295.

10. Part letter from B.F.V. ELSDEN, Solicitor, Littlehampton.

11. Draft letter to Mrs Dixon KIMBER, "Kedish," Knightscroft, (Avenue) Rustington.

12. Pages 5 to 8 of 'The Times' dated 1st June, 1940.

13. Cutting from the 'Daily Mail' 13/2/39.

14. Eight copies of pamphlet "Farmers, you have been doped."

15. Pamphlet "The wicked folly of anti-semitism."

16. Cutting from newspaper - undated.

17. Rubber whip.

18. Bunch of 16 keys and 1 key on white tape.

19. 3 used carbon sheets.

20. Fascist motor car flag.

APPENDIX 4

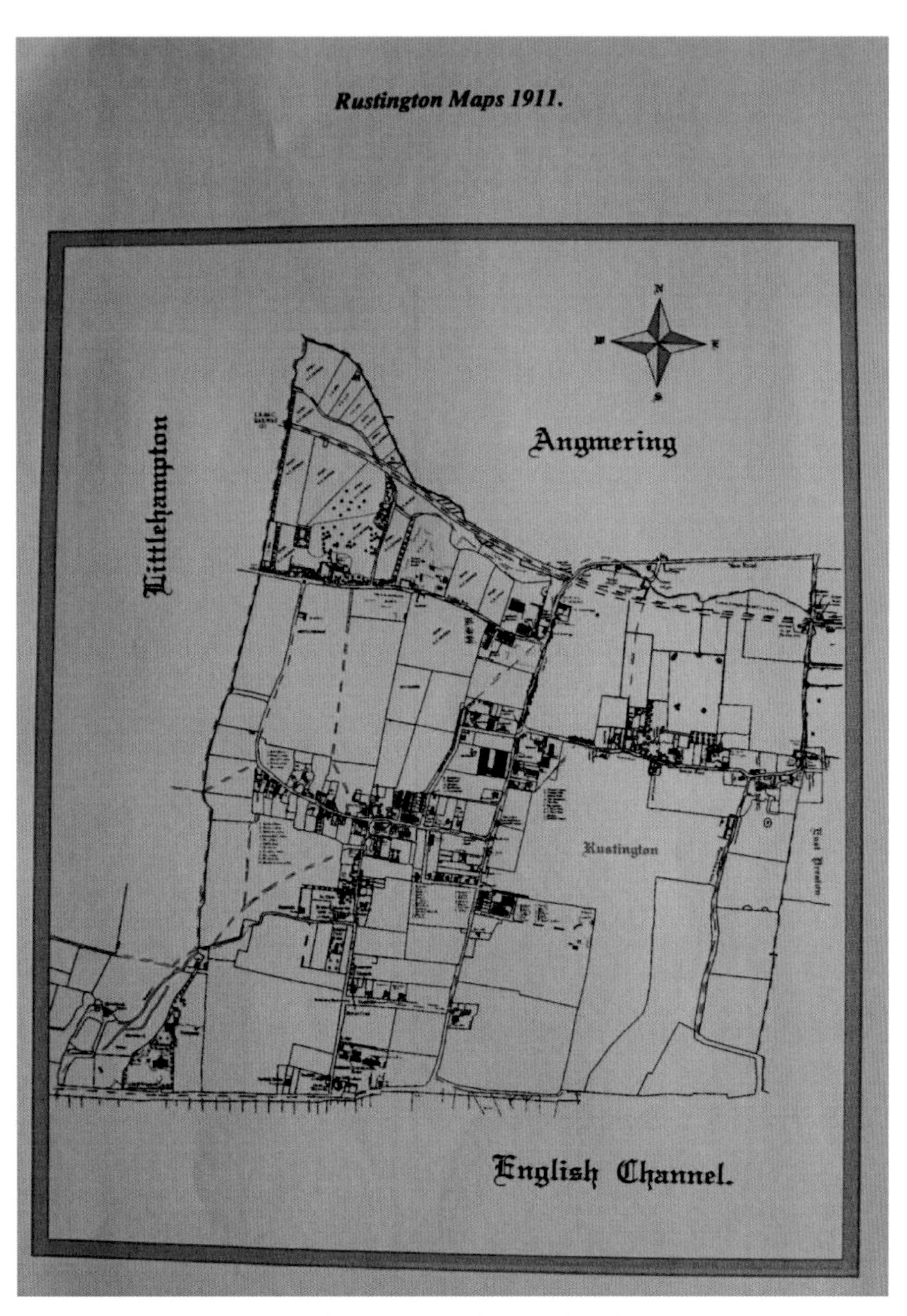

Map showing Rustington in 1911.
The following pages show close ups of each region of the village.

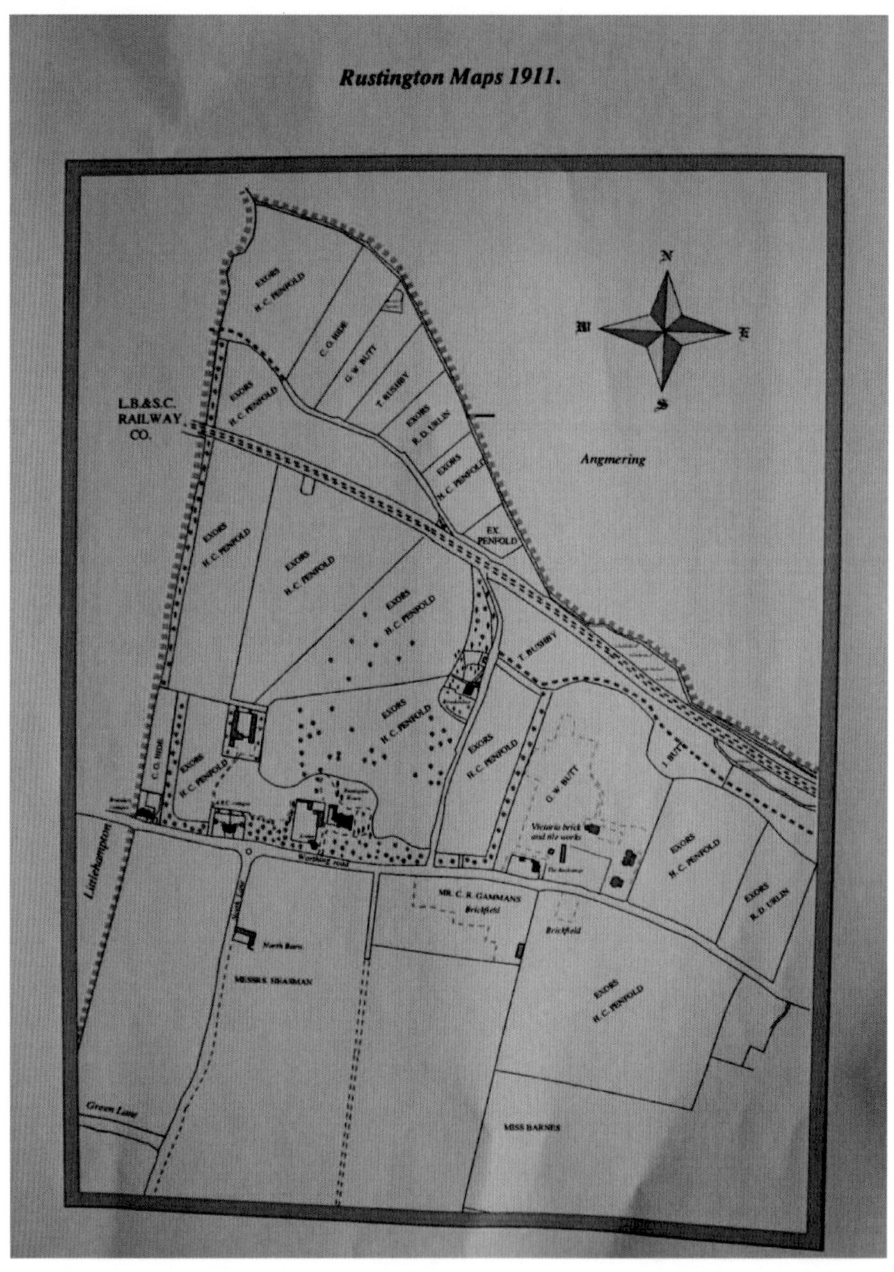

Map showing the properties and landowners in the north-west of Rustington. It shows in the bottom half, North Lane, Worthing Road and the footpath which is now Old Manor Road.

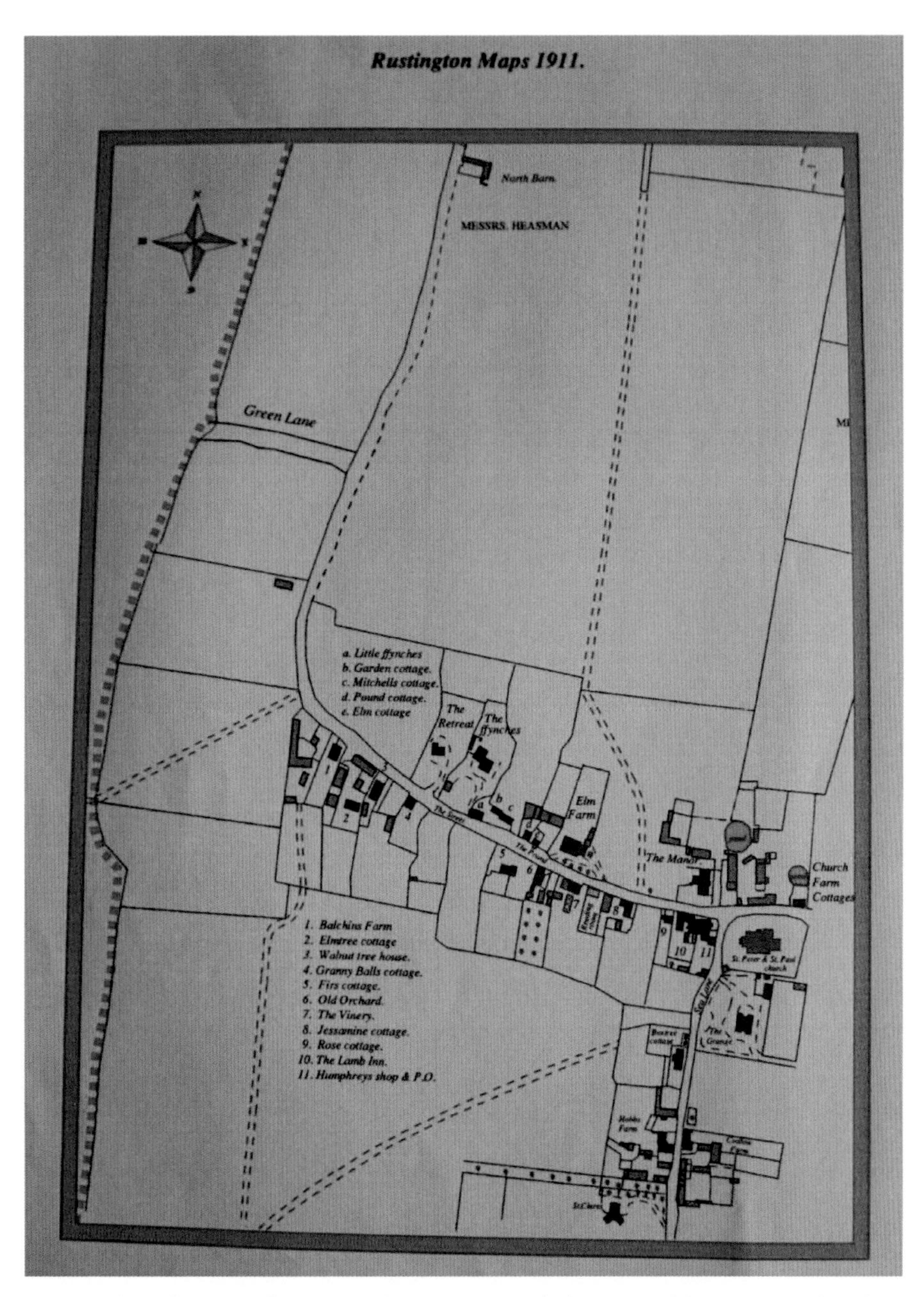

Map showing North Lane, The Street and the top of Sea Lane. On the map No. 6 is The Firs (now Old Orchard) the home of the Garretts, and The Grange just south of the Parish Church.

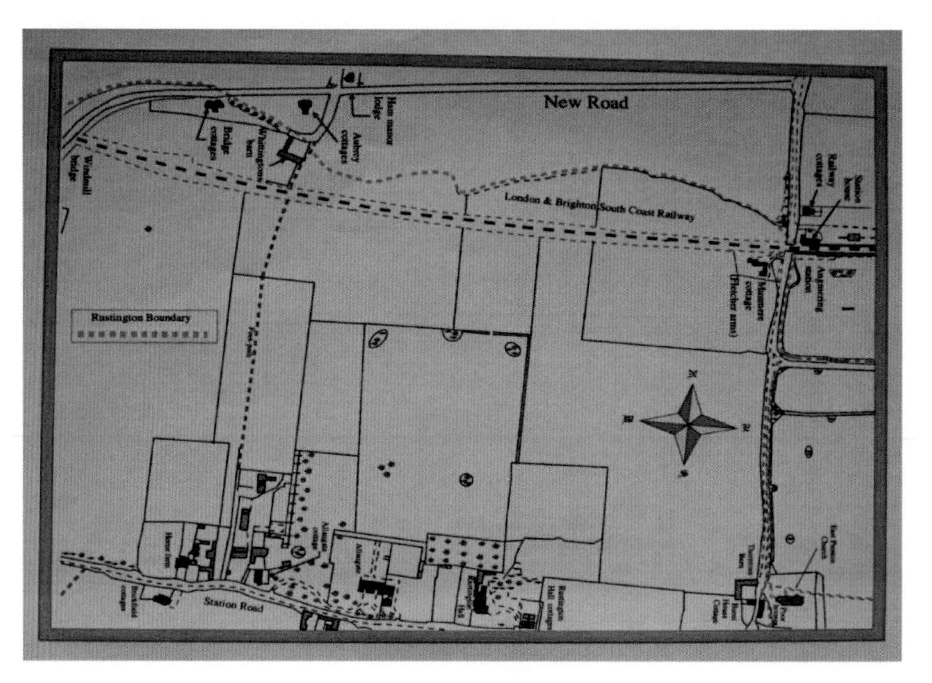

Map of the north-east of Rustington, which shows Allangate and Rustington Hall.

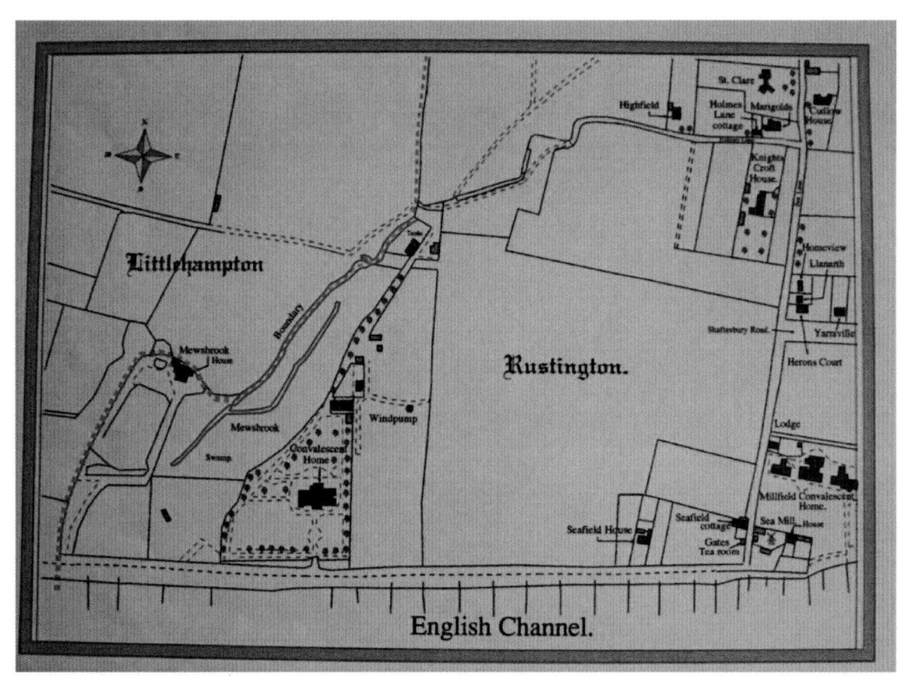

Map showing the bottom of Sea Lane with Cudlow House in the north-east corner where J M Barrie and the Llewelyn Davies family lived with the Parry's house Knightscroft opposite. It also shows the Mill House next to the Sea Mill in the south-east corner and the convalescent home on the Littlehampton border.

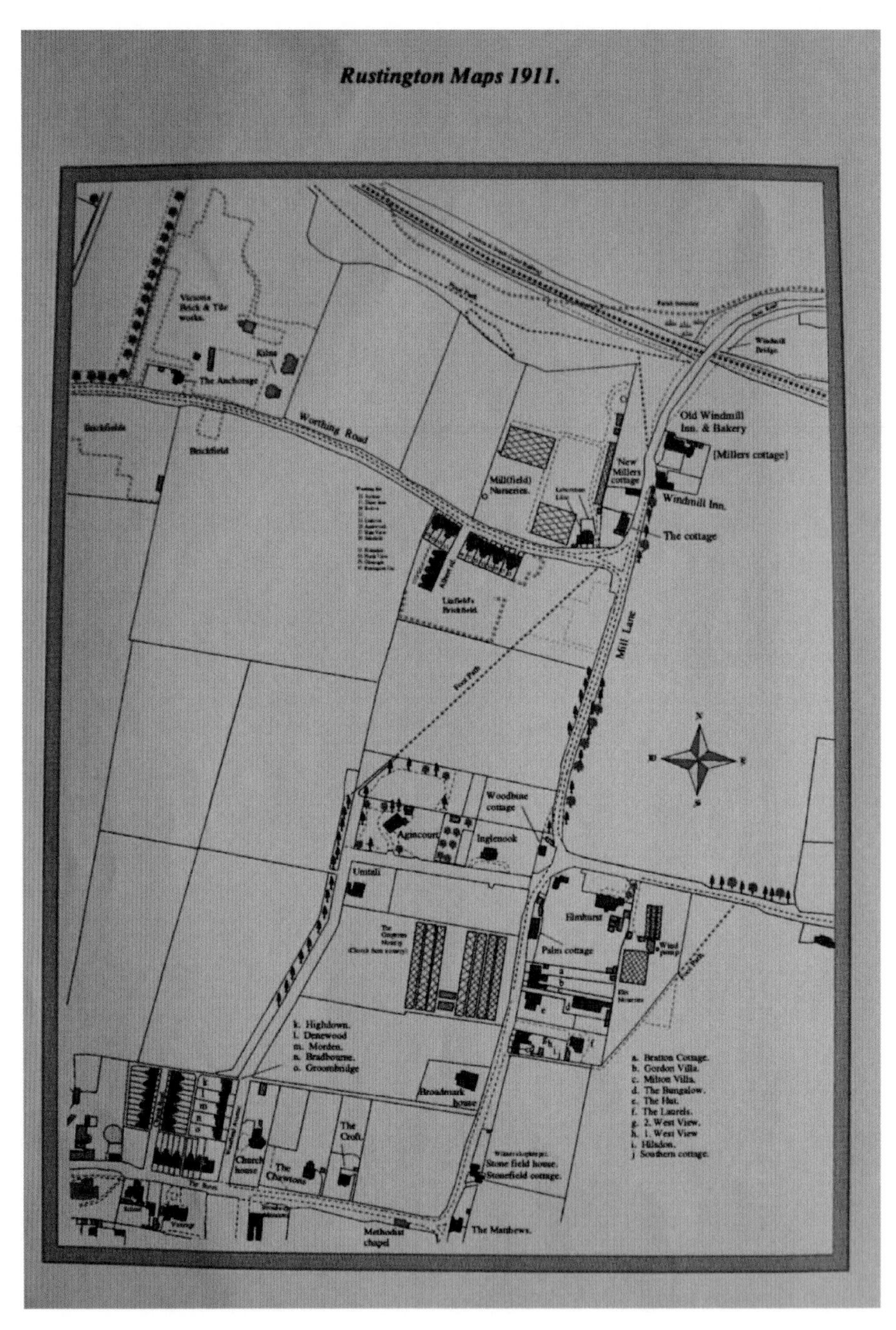

Map showing Abbotswood on the corner of Ash Lane and Station Road. Station Road runs east-west below Mill Lane, and Ash Lane runs north-south below Mill Lane.

APPENDIX 5

Rhoda Garrett death certificate.

CERTIFIED COPY OF AN ENTRY OF DEATH

GIVEN AT THE GENERAL REGISTER OFFICE

Application Number 6021388-1

	REGISTRATION DISTRICT	ST GILES
1882	DEATH in the Sub-district of St Giles North	in the County of Middlesex

Columns:–	1	2	3	4	5	6	7	8	9
No.	When and where died	Name and surname	Sex	Age	Occupation	Cause of death	Signature, description and residence of informant	When registered	Signature of registrar
495	Twenty second November 1882 2 Gower Street	Rhoda Garrett.	Female	40 years	art decorator Daughter of John Fisher Garrett (deceased) Rector of Elton Derbyshire	Typhoid Fever 23 days Bronchitis 12 days Certified by E. G. Anderson M.D. L.S.A. Lond.	Mary Jardine Present at Death 2 Gower Street	Twenty third November 1882	W. B. Peach Registrar

CERTIFIED to be a true copy of an entry in the certified copy of a Register of Deaths in the District above mentioned.

Given at the GENERAL REGISTER OFFICE, under the Seal of the said Office, the 5th day of November 2014

DYD 775368

See note overleaf

CAUTION: THERE ARE OFFENCES RELATING TO FALSIFYING OR ALTERING A CERTIFICATE AND USING OR POSSESSING A FALSE CERTIFICATE ©CROWN COPYRIGHT

WARNING: A CERTIFICATE IS NOT EVIDENCE OF IDENTITY.

LAC

GENERAL REGISTER OFFICE ENGLAND

APPENDIX 6 Simplified Garrett Family Tree

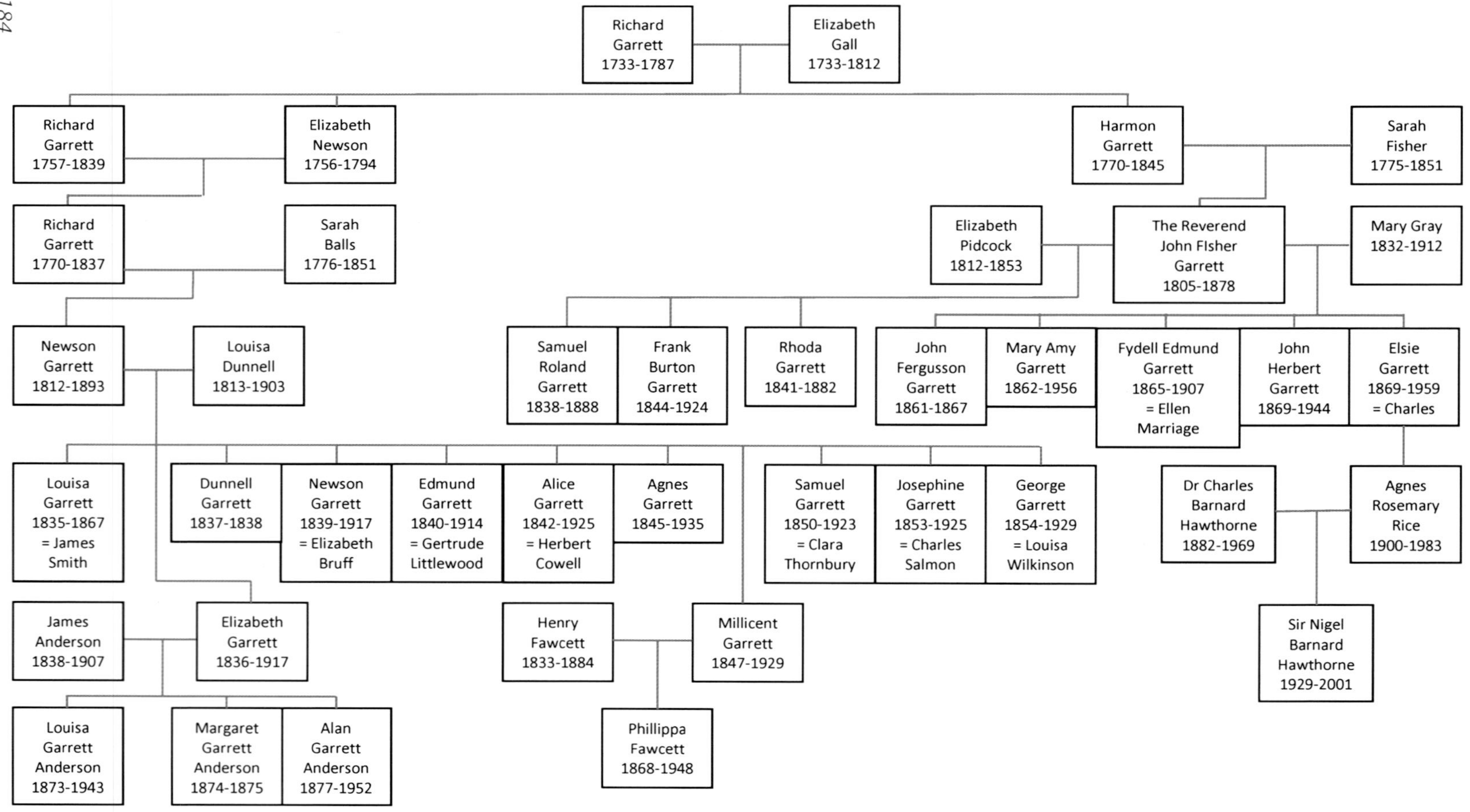

APPENDIX 7 Partial family tree showing the link between Sir Hubert Parry and the Duke and Duchess of Cambridge

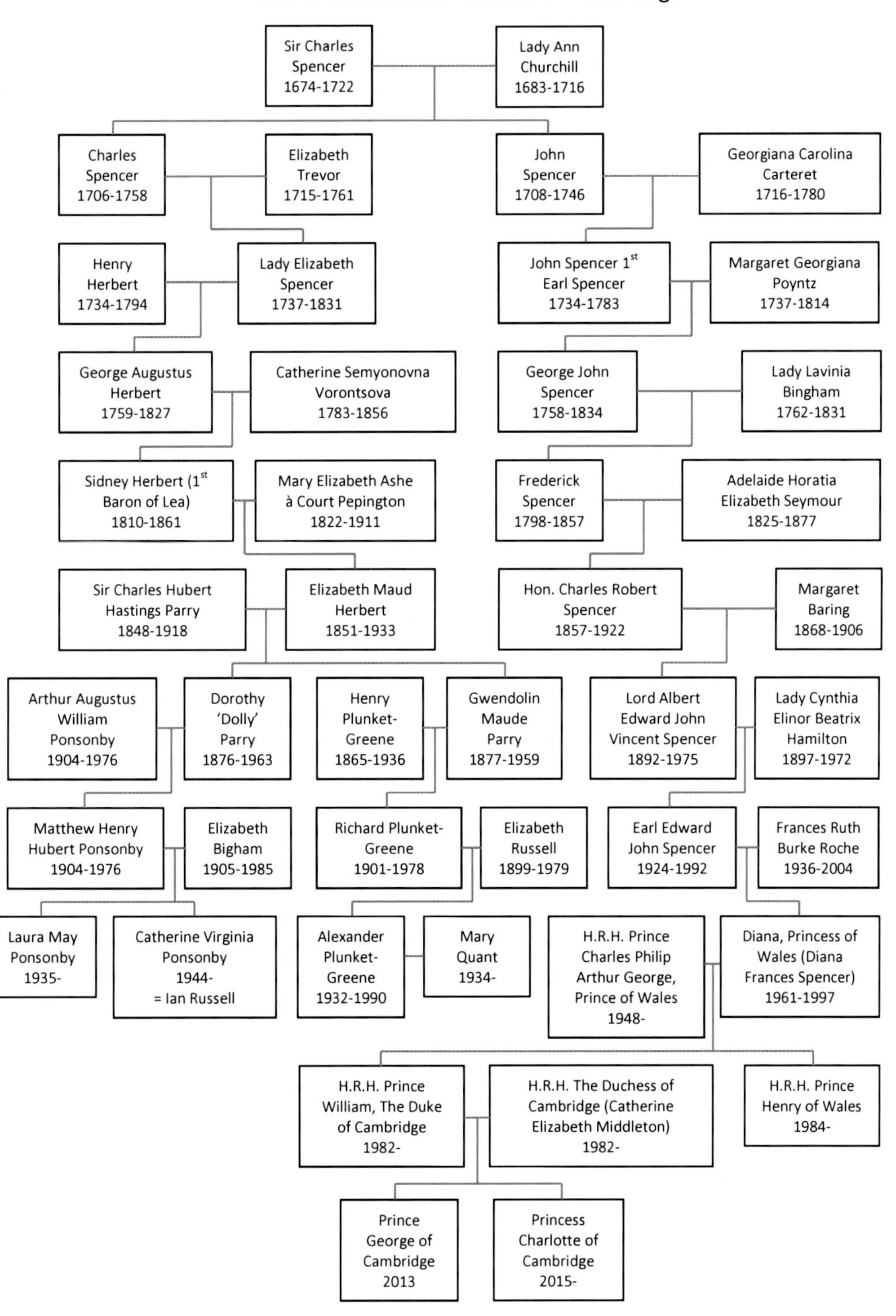

BIBLIOGRAPHY

1881 England Census (database online) (2004). RG11. *Piece: 1119; Folio: 81-92.*

1911 England Census (database online) (2011). RG14. *Piece: 5354; Schedule 126.*

Barrie, J. (1950). *Allahakbarries C.C.* London: J. Barrie Publishers.

Crawford, E. (1999). *The Women's Suffrage Movement in Britain: A Reference Guide 1866-1928.* London: UCL Press.

Crawford, E. (2002). *Enterprising Women: The Garretts and their Circle.* London: Francis Boutle Publishers.

Dundee Courier (1954, December 13). Death of Major-Gen. Sir John Davidson. 2.

Fawcett, M. (1924). *What I Remember.* London: T Fisher Unwin.

Gibson, A. & Chalke, S. (2013). *Gentleman Gypsies and Jesters – The Wonderful World of Cricket.* Bath: Fairfield Books.

Hannah, I. (1912). *The Sussex Coast.* London: T Fisher Unwin.

Hennessey, B. (2005). *The Emergence of Broadcasting in Britain.* Lympstone: Southerleigh.

Hollis, W. M. (1918, April). Women's Suffrage in Editorial. *Scribble*, p.4.

Hollis, W. M. (1918, April). Women's Suffrage. *Scribble*, p.11.

http://www.digplanet.com/wiki/Thomas Shaw (MP). (2014, October 22).

Leeds Mercury. (1885, February 10). Concert in the Albert

Hall. 8.

Littlehampton News. (1891, September 15). Robin Society at Rustington. 2.

Littlehampton News. (1893, October). Opening of the new Rustington Reading Room.

MacMillan, A. (2000). *Mauritius Illustrated Historical and Descriptive Commercial and Industrial Facts, Figures and Resources.* Reprint London Edition: Asian Educational Services.

Portsmouth Evening News. (1893, February 10). By-Election. *The Result at Halifax*, 2.

Poulton, D. (2013). *The Lady with the Lute.* Norwich: Smokehouse Press.

Sharp, E. (1933). *Unfinished Adventure.* London: John Lane.

Simkins, M. (2008). *Fatty Batter.* London: Ebury Press.

Southampton University (2013). Mrs Diana Bailey: Friend. *Parkes Annual Review 2012-13*, p. 24.

Smythe, D. E. (1919). *Impressions that Remained.* London: Longmans, Green & Co.

The Littlehampton Observer. (1914, October 21). Patriotic Concert at Rustington. 2.

The National Archives, Kew. (1940-1945). WAR: John Sidney George Crosland (associate of William Joyce), detained under Defence Regulation 18B. *HO 144/22158.*

The News & South Coast Visitors Journal. (1887, October 26). Madam Melba. 2.

Urlin, M. (1909). *The Journal and Reminiscences of R Denny Urlin.* Letchworth: Arden Press.

Yorkshire Evening Post. (1934, November 14). *Vicar Supports Fascists.* 13.

PHOTOGRAPHS AND MAPS

We wish to thank the following people for allowing us to use the photographs as follows:

Diana Bailey: 106; 107; 109-111; 120.

Huw Stephenson: 14-17; 19; 22; 28; 30-32.

Topical Press Agency/Getty Images: 12

Andy Kyte: 126; 127.

Laura Ponsonby: 26-27; 39.

Courtesy of Great Ormond Street Hospital Children's Charity: 54-57; 59; 60; 62; 64-66.

All other photographs have come from the authors' collection as follows:

Graeme's collection: 1; 2; 3; 18; 20; 21; 24; 25; 29; 34; 35; 40; 41; 46; 50; 51; 67-69; 71; 77-79; 81; 85; 86; 90; 95; 96; 105; 112-114; 119; 121; 128-130.

Mary and Bev's collection: 4-11; 13; 23; 33; 36-38; 42-45; 47-49; 52; 53; 58; 61; 63; 70; 72-76; 80; 82-84; 87-89; 91-94; 97-104; 108; 115-118; 122-125.

All maps courtesy of Bev Taylor.

ACKNOWLEDGEMENTS

This book has been based on extensive research that we have undertaken on the people, places and events occurring in Rustington from Victorian times to the present date.

We would like to thank the following people who have either inspired us, encouraged us to start the project, obtained information for the contents, helped us to persevere with the book and finally to publish the works.

As we said in the Introduction, the idea for this collaboration came from a visit to a Focus concert at Trading Boundaries, Fletching, near Sheffield Park and the Bluebell Railway. Trading Boundaries is not just a live music venue and gallery, housing the magnificent artwork/paintings of Roger Dean, but it also has a café and a variety of shops all set in a beautiful Georgian manor house. So we would firstly like to thank the owners of this fantastic venue, Tracy Thompson and Michael Clifford and all the staff for making our visits so enjoyable. We cannot go further without thanking the brilliant Thijs van Leer, Pierre van der Linden, Menno Gootjes and Bobby Jacobs from our favourite band, Focus, for their wonderful music, not forgetting the lovely Anne-Lies.

We now move onto the contents of the book, where we would like to especially thank Laura Ponsonby and Kate & Ian Russell at Shulbrede Priory for their wonderful hospitality and allowing us to peruse the diaries of Sir Hubert Parry, Lady Maude and their daughter Dolly Ponsonby, which have proved to be an invaluable source of information with regard to the Parry family and their close friends the Garretts, and we thank them also for the use of photographs and sketches held in their collection.

We also wish to thank Elizabeth Crawford for further information regarding the Garrett family and for contacting members of the wider Garrett family to enable us to use further photographs for our publication. In this respect we'd like to thank Hew Stephenson.

A big thank to Jessica Petit, curator of Rustington Museum and to Christine De Poortere, Peter Pan director for the Great Ormond Street Hospital Children's Charity for their help with the JM Barrie chapter.

A special mention we'd like to make is to James Turner for his extensive research into the Rawson-Shaw family, Davidson family and the Croslands for the 'Gentleman Vicar and the Controversial Vicar' chapter; it has been a great help.

In regards to the chapter on 'Fascism comes to Rustington' we wish to extend our hearty thanks to Diana Bailey for her kind hospitality and the incredible amount of information and pictures regarding both her family and that of the Croslands.

For the chapter on 'The Special Wireless Service' we would like to thank Andy Kyte.

Graeme would also like to thank all his Baldwins' cricket colleagues both past and present, too numerous to mention all individually. However, there are a few we would like to mention in particular, firstly, to the late Rod Suddaby for the initial motivation and advice he gave to me on the newly-released material from the National Archives; to John Bunker for first introducing me to the Baldwins; also to our President, Michael Simkins, author of the book *Fatty Batter*; and a special thank you to Professor Peter Swaab for advising me 'not to hold back' and 'go for it' and giving me the courage to continue at our latest cricket dinner. I have made many friends there and I wish to thank you all.

Mum and I would like to offer our heartfelt thanks to Jag Lall, our book cover designer; Ian Large, our copy editor; and Graham Cook of Writersworld for making the whole process of publishing our book so smooth.

There are certain people without whom this book would not have been possible at all, our family.

To my brother Dr Andrew Taylor, Nicky and their family.

To my children, Bethany, Iain and Edward for putting up with my constant talk about this book and the characters therein.

To Dad, thank you for the maps hand-drawn in the appendices and other photographs and items from your collection and to Mum without whom none of this would have been possible!

Finally, there is one person to whom we owe a huge thank you and that is my wife Sue for her excellent proof reading of our various drafts as well as her patience with us over the amount of time we have had to spend on the book!

I dedicate this book to you all!

Graeme

I must give my heartfelt grateful thanks to dear Graeme, for when he more or less took over writing and researching for this book, after a compression fracture of my spine stopped me in my tracks. His encouragement and interest enabled us to work together, travel together as far Pershore near Worcester, Kew Public Record Office, Shulbrede Priory, The Priory at Cross-in-Hand, Froxfield Green, Petersfield and London, where we have met the most interesting people in order to obtain the necessary information and photographs we needed to complete the publication. He then discovered in himself the ability to write this interesting and informative book.

Congratulations Graeme.

Mum

Answer: A missing 20th item!

PRINTED AND BOUND BY:

Copytech (UK) Limited trading as Printondemand-worldwide,
9 Culley Court, Bakewell Road, Orton Southgate. Peterborough,
PE2 6XD, United Kingdom.